the Moral
Machinery

*"God would have His servants become acquainted
with the moral machinery of their own hearts..."*

by
Dan Vis

ISBN: 978-0-9821805-1-8

Published by FAST Missions
P.O. Box 1842
Batavia, IL 60510

Additional copies of this book are available by calling toll free
1-800-501-4024 or visiting WWW.FAST.ST

Cover design by Tara Gieck
Editing by Marilyn Morgan

Printed by Remnant Publications,
Coldwater, Michigan
United States of America

Dedication

This book is dedicated to Vi and Becca. To Vi, for repeatedly challenging me to put some training on character into print. To Becca, for being a constant encouragement that these principles were worth printing. Thank you, with much love.

Special Thanks

To the North Aurora church for giving me the wonderful opportunity to come and minister in your midst. And for your kind and loving acceptance of my family and me.

To David and Beverly Sedlacek, Ric and Jane Espana, Wayne and Jeanine Allen, Robert Terrelonge, and others who have personally helped me better understand the moral machinery.

To Jesus Christ, for having reached down into the innermost chamber of my heart, and igniting there a small flicker of glory.

Table of Contents

Preface: The Moral Machinery 1

Chapter 1:   The Hidden Blueprint 3

Chapter 2:   First Principles   12

Chapter 3:   Battle for the Mind 31

Chapter 4:   Power for Victory 58

Chapter 5:   Understanding Character 76

Chapter 6:   Life in the Spirit 98

Chapter 7:   The Quest 124

Appendix: About the Sanctuary 134

The Moral Machinery
Preface

It was one of those moments where you sense God is speaking directly to your heart. The setting was British Columbia, Canada. On a remote island in the middle of a sparkling blue lake. Nothing around but trees, a pebble-strewn beach, and the sound of lapping waves. I had been invited up to spend a weekend with a team of Bible workers doing some of the most innovative and cutting-edge ministry anywhere in North America. They were about ready to launch a new year of evangelism, and the team was having a special wilderness retreat in preparation for the busy schedule of upcoming events. I had been invited along to give a few devotional talks.

For my theme, I chose to cover the topics presented in this book. It was not all fully formulated in my mind at the time, but there was enough to get us thinking. Using a stick, I had scraped out a sketch of the Old Testament sanctuary on the ground, and had been exploring what it suggested about the workings of the human mind. The moral machinery, so to speak. The quietness of conviction was clearly settling in as each grappled with the implications. Finally, my close friend, the director of the ministry, spoke up: "What this really means, Dan, is we need a whole new breed of worker!"

That's when I heard God speaking. The words riveted themselves in my mind. Of course--it has to be! If we are serious about finishing the work, it is going to take a whole new breed of worker. Workers with far more insight into the inner workings of the human heart. Who truly grasp the keys to victory over temptation. Who live with a profound sensitivity to the promptings of the Spirit. Who experience a richer, almost radical, level of spirituality. To finish the work, we have got to get down to understanding the nitty gritty of how Christianity works. It is going to take nothing less!

Well, that's the prayer of this book. That God will use it to help raise up a whole new breed of worker. Men and women who understand the moral machinery. It is not a finished work, by any means. It feels more like a first stab at a whole new field of research. Others have hinted around the edges, but this work dives in full force. And pioneers rarely get everything right the first time. Rather, they break new ground. Raise questions. Challenge assumptions. Shake things up. Those who come after fill in the pieces, correct the mistakes, and polish the rough edges. If this work generates some good discussion, stimulates our thinking, and helps even a few to enjoy a deeper walk with God, it will have been worth the effort. But if it sparks a movement of more Spirit-filled men and women, more effective workers who will live wholly for God in these trying times, it will fulfil its purpose. That's what I'm really after. That's my prayer.

So much for the preface. You are about to launch into a fascinating study of the moral machinery. We'll soon be peering deep inside the hidden mysteries of the human heart. Buckle up, and get ready. . .

The Hidden Blueprint
Chapter 1

*What? know ye not that your body is
the temple of the Holy Ghost which is in you,
which ye have of God, and ye are not your own?
For ye are bought with a price: therefore glorify God
in your body, and in your spirit, which are God's.
I Corinthians 6:19-20*

Words. They can be a bit problematic at times, can't they? How many times have you strung a few of them together to try and communicate some idea, only to have your listener interpret them quite differently from what you intended? It has probably happened to all of us. Even God has had some difficulty in this area: consider the hundreds of Christian denominations today, each with their own unique creed based on some different interpretation of the exact same words–the Bible. Astonishing, actually.

Or we scratch our head trying to conjure up just the right word to express some idea, and we draw a blank. Sometimes it's just a momentary glitch in our memory. But more often than not, the exact word simply doesn't exist. What do we do then?

Take the word "character." Arguably it is one of the most import concepts in the Bible. Much of our personal happiness and success in life is tied up with the character we form, or fail to form. The plan of salvation involves restoring fallen men and women back to a righteous character. And we often talk with longing about the day Christ's character will be reproduced in His church–without spot or wrinkle–so He can come and take us home to be with Him. In fact, the whole great controversy between Christ and Satan, waged these last 6000 years, has been largely an argument over the character of God. Character is everywhere! There's only one problem: the word doesn't appear once in the Bible.

Of course, the need to understand character is more urgent now than ever. The cancer of sin has metastasized to every level of society, slowly but insidiously, sapping the last vestiges of integrity and morality out of our culture: media and entertainment, corruption in politics, sensuality and immorality, anger and violence, and worse. It is everywhere. What we need are men and women of character–ready to stand for God in these perilous last days. Where are they?

Actually, "character" is not our only problem word. Even common biblical terms, like spirit, sin, soul, faith, heart, flesh, and conscience frequently get thrown around by Christians, without much careful analysis. And because they are poorly defined, and vaguely understood, we often come to confused conclusions. While vitally important concepts, our understanding of them is often fuzzy at best. Until we dig a little deeper into the meaning of some of these words, we are not likely to get very far in our understanding of character.

LOST IN ARKANSAS

When our daughter began getting close to high school age, my wife and I started looking for a Christian school to give her the kind of character training we valued. One school that interested us was found a couple states over, in Arkansas. Another family we worked with, had a daughter the same age–so we decided to caravan together and visit the school, for a first-hand look.

Neither of us had been there before. And it was located in a secluded, rural area–deliberately off the beaten path–no doubt to discourage worldly influences. My friend had scribbled down a few directions on how to get there and was leading the way. We followed in our car.

To make a long story short–we took a wrong turn somewhere. We were in the right general vicinity, when we noticed the road began to change. It started getting narrower and narrower. It switched from pavement to gravel, and then soon to plain old dirt. We ended up out in the middle of a field, and then the road just quit completely. We were totally lost–there wasn't a house in sight, much less a street sign. Just having a few directions wasn't really enough, what we needed was a map.[1]

As Christians we often limp along like this, trying to follow some hurriedly scribbled instructions (those common cliches we share with one another), but without any real map of the moral machinery inside of us. We have a vague sense of man's various faculties, but don't really understand how they are supposed to work, or how they interrelate with each other. When struggling with temptation–we don't really understand what is happening or what we are supposed to do. Others may

---

1. *This was in the days before GPS systems were widely available. As we will see in the pages ahead, God not only gives us a map of man's moral machinery, but a fully functional turn-by-turn GPS directional system. "thine ears shall hear a word behind thee, saying, This is the way, walk ye in it." Isaiah 30:21*

offer a suggestion here or there, but they are often of limited value. So we limp along managing the best we can, wondering if everyone else struggles like we do! [2]

Our understanding of many common theological concepts such as conversion, sanctification, and of course character development, would also benefit from some kind of spiritual map. One that enabled us to actually understand the internal faculties involved in conversion. The mechanics of sanctification. The process by which character is transformed. Rather than a haphazardly collected grab bag of tips and tricks, what if we actually understood the interactions of the various faculties like reason, the will, faith, the conscience, emotions and the rest. What if all these faculties could be laid out before our eyes like a map?

KNOW YE NOT...

Actually, they can. The Bible lays out what appears to be an amazing blueprint of the entire inner machinery, in the Old Testament sanctuary or tabernacle.[3] And then it calls our attention to this blueprint repeatedly. To be honest, I don't

---

2. When we run into someone struggling with depression, anxiety, some phobia, or any other serious mental health issue, we are even less able to help. So we send them off to a specialist, who tries to treat them using some map or model of how the mind works, drawn from years of study at a secular university. And with mixed results. What if Christians had a map of their own? One drawn directly from the Bible? Would we be better able, perhaps, to begin helping those struggling with these kinds of problems?

3. Initially, the sanctuary was a large tent built in the wilderness by the ancient Hebrews shortly after escaping Egypt. Also called the tabernacle, this tent was later replaced by a majestic temple during the reign of King Solomon. For more information, and a simple sketch of the sanctuary, see the appendix at the end of this book.

know how I missed the link for so long! Evidently some in Paul's day failed to make the connection as well. Take this familiar verse for example:

> *Know ye not that ye are the temple of God, and that the Spirit of God dwelleth in you? I Corinthians 3:16*

Just as the Shekinah Glory filled the Most Holy Place of the Old Testament sanctuary, so God intends for the Spirit of God to come into each of our lives as believers, into the very core of our being. We are all a temple. Every one of us, individually. That Old Testament sanctuary is a map of you!

A few chapters later Paul repeats the idea. And once again, we are pointed back to the sanctuary to understand what it means to be a Christian.

> *What? know ye not that your body is the temple of the Holy Ghost which is in you, which ye have of God, and ye are not your own? For ye are bought with a price: therefore glorify God in your body, and in your spirit, which are God's. I Corinthians 6:19-20.*

The sanctuary is a picture of how the Spirit of God comes into our life. We tend to connect these verses primarily with diet and exercise, or some other aspect of physical health. But the passage calls us to glorify God both physically and spiritually. In fact, the emphasis seems to be on the latter. In the context, Paul is talking about immorality.

These aren't the only places this connection can be seen. In II Corinthians 5:1, Paul refers to our bodies as the "earthly house of this tabernacle" and hints at the future "building of God" awaiting us "eternal in the heavens." Peter, likewise, clearly links our body to the sanctuary: "Yea, I think it meet, as long as I am in this tabernacle, to stir you up by putting you in remembrance; knowing that shortly I must put off this my tabernacle, even as our Lord Jesus Christ hath shewed me" (II Peter 1:13-14).

Not surprisingly, Jesus Himself, taught the same idea. When asked for a sign He was the Messiah, He answered: "Destroy this temple, and in three days I will raise it up." Then John explains, "But he spake of the temple of his body" (John 2:19-21). Clearly, Jesus understood the close link between the temple and man's moral machinery. He knew His body was a living temple, filled with the Shekinah Glory.

And note this detail from Revelation's description of the New Jerusalem: "I saw no temple therein: for the Lord God Almighty and the Lamb are the temple of it" (Revelation 21:22). Not only is man a temple–but God is too! Which makes sense when we remember that man was made in the image of God (Genesis 1:26). In short, if we want to understand how God has made us, and the inner workings of our moral machinery, we should expect to be able to glean at least some information from this Old Testament building. It's certainly worth a closer look.

THY WAY, O GOD

In fact, I'm convinced this was God's primary purpose for the sanctuary all along. When first giving Moses instructions about how to build it there in the wilderness around Mount Sinai, God gave this explanation of its purpose: "And let them make me a sanctuary; that I may dwell among them" (Exodus 25:8). Now God didn't need a building in order to dwell in their midst. He had been present in the pillar of fire and cloud of smoke ever since leaving Egypt. Rather, He wanted to dwell among them in a deeper way, within their hearts. And He gave them the building to teach them how this happens. How the Spirit of God comes to dwell inside a man. As the Psalmist put it: "thy way, O God, is in the sanctuary" (Psalms 77:13). God's plan for living Spirit-filled lives is encoded in this Old Testament symbol. Unfortunately today, much like then, few discern the instruction God intends from that old tent they hauled through the desert.

I had been studying this subject for some time, and begun to notice many of the parallels between the sanctuary and what the Bible teaches about man's moral machinery, when I stumbled on to an amazing statement. It was in a book discussing biblical principles of education–in a chapter examining God's methods for instructing the children of Israel just after delivering them from long years of degrading slavery. In particular, it highlighted the sanctuary system. Here's the statement:

> *Through Christ was to be fulfilled the purpose of which the tabernacle was a symbol–that glorious building, its walls of glistening gold reflecting in rainbow hues the curtains inwrought with cherubim, the fragrance of ever-burning incense pervading all, the priests robed in spotless white, and in the deep mystery of the inner place, above the mercy seat, between the figures of the bowed, worshiping angels, the glory of the Holiest. In all, God desired His people to read His purpose for the human soul.*

The statement goes on to indicate what that purpose was: "It was the same purpose long afterward set forth by the apostle Paul, speaking by the Holy Spirit: 'Know ye not that ye are the temple of God, and that the Spirit of God dwelleth in you?'"[4] The goal of the sanctuary was to teach us how to live a Spirit-filled life!

According to the author, everything in the sanctuary, down to the most striking details, was intended for us to understand something about the human soul, and God's purpose for it. The purpose exemplified and lived out in Christ. To grasp that purpose, and how to cooperate with God in its fulfillment, we must learn to read these lessons in the sanctuary.

In the pages ahead we will attempt to do just that. We will use the sanctuary as a blueprint for how God has made us, and how the various faculties of our moral machinery work together. In so doing, a whole new field of study will open to our understanding. We will discover extraordinary parallels, answers to many important questions, and more important, keys to Spirit-filled living. How to have the Shekinah Glory burning bright in the sanctuary of our individual hearts. If this is the desire of your heart, keep reading. . .

---

4. *Education, p. 36.*

Review Questions
Chapter 1–The Hidden Blueprint

1.　　*Why are men and women of character needed so urgently today? Why are they so uncommon?*

2.　　*How can a map of man's moral machinery help us understand the Christian life more fully?*

3.　　*What did God intend for His people to learn from the sanctuary?*

4.　　*Give examples from the Bible of how God calls our attention to the sanctuary to understand human nature.*

5.　　*What is God's ultimate purpose for the human soul?*

First Principles
Chapter 2

And the very God of peace sanctify you wholly;
and I pray God your whole spirit and soul and body
be preserved blameless unto the coming
of our Lord Jesus Christ. Faithful is he
that calleth you, who also will do it.
I Thessalonians 5:23-24

Before launching our exploration of the sanctuary, I'd like to ask one favor: hear me out. Give me a chance to present the evidence before discarding the thesis of the book. We are going to cover a surprizingly broad range of topics–and because so many have "fuzzy" ideas in at least some of these areas, it is almost certain something ahead will cross a pre-conceived idea or assumption. Keep reading, and things should gradually come into focus. But it will take some time to lay out the entire map. Thank you in advance for this courtesy!

* * * * * * *

My wife and I recently celebrated a wonderful open house at a ministry we were associated with. When we first began working there, the building was nothing more than a large concrete slab and a few steel girders. Gradually over the course of the next few years, our small team of builders put up the roof, the walls, wiring, plumbing, and vents. Then came the furnishings and decor. At every step, God provided the means to make it possible. And little by little the building took shape, until finally we were able to open the doors and begin using our beautiful, brand new facility.[5] It was a wonderful and exciting day! But it all began with a rolled up scroll of paper containing the floor plans for the building.

In studying the sanctuary, we too must begin with an exploration of the floor plan. The sanctuary was basically divided into three main sections. First, an area outside the building surrounded by a screen of white linen all the way around called the Outer Court. Then inside, the building was divided into two additional sections, called the Holy Place where most of the day to day temple activity occurred, and the Most Holy Place, where only the High Priest could go. And then, only once a year for a special, sacred service on the Day of Atonement. Three partitions–two inside, and one out.

How did God create man? Remarkably similar. Notice the three divisions suggested in Paul's prayer:

> *And the very God of peace sanctify you wholly, and I pray God your whole spirit and soul and body be preserved blameless unto the coming of our Lord Jesus Christ.*
> *I Thessalonians 5:23*

---

5. *The building was a small lifestyle center, designed to help people regain health naturally from chronic degenerative diseases, using simple means in harmony with Scripture. For more information, visit www.ucheepines.org.*

To be sanctified "wholly" three regions must be "preserved blameless": our spirit, soul, and body. Two on the inside, and one on the outside. Just like the sanctuary. We will analyze these words more carefully in a few moments, but for now, just notice the similarity.

THE OUTER COURT

Take a moment to reflect on the Outer Court. In many ways, it parallels our physical body. A white linen screen was wrapped around the entire perimeter of the Outer Court, with only one opening, just before the entrance to the building proper. It is not so different from the clothes we wrap around ourselves, to cover our bodies (more or less[6]), leaving the primary entrances to our inner man–the sense organs of our face and hands–uncovered.

The white linen also seems to point to the actions we take with our bodies. In Revelation 19:8 we find these words: "And to her [the bride] was granted that she should be arrayed in fine linen, clean and white: for the fine linen is the righteousness of saints." God's plan is for our life to be one of constant right-doing. A covering of white raiment. The choice to do right, of course comes from within, and the power comes from Christ. But it is the body that executes that decision. As Deuteronomy 6:25 puts it: "And it shall be our righteousness, if we *observe to do* all these commandments before the LORD our God, as he hath commanded us."

---

6. *Of course, immodesty has become a serious problem in contemporary society. The sanctuary suggests appropriately covering our body is a part of God's plan for our life. Cultural trends, unfortunately, are leading us in the opposite direction.*

Of course, only one person has ever lived a perfect life of spotless white: Jesus Christ. He alone, fulfilled God's purpose for human life, as depicted in the sanctuary. In contrast, all of us have done things we regret, that we knew were not right. Our righteousness, apart from Christ, is as "filthy rags" (Isaiah 64:6). Thankfully, there is forgiveness in Christ. "Though your sins be as scarlet, they shall be as white as snow" (Isaiah 1:18) there is the hope of cleansing, by "the washing of water by the word" (Ephesians 5:26). We will study this topic more fully in a future chapter.

IN HEAVENLY PLACES

Going back to the book of Revelation we find the following interesting comment about the Outer Court. Notice Revelation 11:1-2:

> *And there was given me a reed like unto a rod: and the angel stood, saying, Rise, and measure the temple of God, and the altar, and them that worship therein. But the court which is without the temple leave out, and measure it not; for it is given unto the Gentiles: and the holy city shall they tread under foot forty and two months.*

While we do not have time to fully explore the prophetic symbolism involved in these verses, it is interesting to note that God's focus is on measuring the inside of the temple–and not the outside. I Samuel 16:7 immediately comes to mind: "the LORD seeth not as man seeth; for man looketh on the outward appearance, but the LORD looketh on the heart."

We are also given the reason–the Outer Court is given unto the Gentiles, who have been allowed to trample it under their feet. Sadly, throughout the history of the church, there has been much persecution: arrests, imprisonment, torture, deprivation, and even executions. All these things are done to the body. The Outer Court. But while others may mistreat us physically, no one can touch what is inside without our consent. It is possible to keep our minds focused on spiritual realities: "If ye then be risen with Christ, seek those things which are above, where Christ sitteth on the right hand of God. Set your affection on things above, not on things on the earth. For ye are dead, and your life is hid with Christ in God" (Colossians 3:1-3).

DIVIDING ASUNDER

If the Outer Court represents our exterior physical body, then the two inner compartments of the sanctuary suggests there are two divisions in the "inner man." That is, the Holy Place and the Most Holy Place suggest two specific interior regions of the moral machinery–each with specific faculties and functions. And what the sanctuary suggests, Paul confirms in his reference to both "soul" and "spirit."[7] The question arises, which part is which? And what do these words really mean, anyway?

One difficulty here is that we cannot simply open up a person's skull and see their moral processes at work. The "machinery" we are talking about is not physiological. It involves faculties and interactions that cannot be detected with scientific instruments. As a result, our only hope is to have God reveal this information to us. Fortunately God has promised to do just that!

---

7. As noted earlier, in I Thessalonians 5:23. There Paul refers to the body, soul and spirit, as the three divisions that must be preserved blameless, if we are to be sanctified wholly.

Notice this claim from the book of Hebrews: "For the word of God is quick, and powerful, and sharper than any twoedged sword, piercing even to the dividing asunder of soul and spirit" (Hebrews 4:12).[8] In other words, the Bible is so precise, we can use it to distinguish between what is soul and what is spirit. It is able to divide them asunder! Furthermore, a careful study of the Bible will enable us to understand which specific faculties are connected with each! But now we are getting ahead of ourselves. . .

THE HOLY PLACE

Let's begin by talking about the word soul. For reasons that will become obvious soon enough, it makes sense to connect this with the Holy Place. Later we will talk about man's spirit and connect that with the Most Holy Place.

I suppose some will object immediately to the idea man has a soul–arguing instead that man is a soul. In Genesis 2:7 for example, we read "And the LORD God formed man of the dust of the ground [his body], and breathed into his nostrils the breath of life [his spirit]; and man became a living soul." This clearly seems to suggest that the soul is the combination of body and spirit–not some third division! Or take Ezekiel 18:4. When God says "the soul that sinneth, it shall die" it sure sounds like He's talking about the entire person, not just some inner partition within man.

---

8. Later in the verse, Paul seems to parallel the soul and spirit with the joints and marrow. Interestingly, the joints are where movement takes place, and the marrow is the source of life-giving blood cells. Similarly, decisions takes place in the soul, but the essence of life issues forth from the spirit. Or as the last part of the verse suggests, the soul consists of our conscious "thoughts" while the spirit consists of the deeper, often unknown "intents of the heart."

The problem, as noted at the beginning of this book, has to do with words. Both of these verses, and others like them, are all found in the Old Testament. They are translated from the Hebrew word–*Nephesh*–which does indeed generally refer to the whole person.[9] But Paul's use of the word soul comes from the New Testament. There it is translated from a Greek word–*Psuche*–which is used quite differently. In other words, the KJV version of the Bible uses the exact same English word "soul" to translate two different words from two different languages, with very different meanings. A sure recipe for confusion!

So what does the Greek word mean then? If it looks familiar, it is–because we have several English words derived from it: psychology, psychiatry, psychosis. These all give us a clue. In fact, we even have an almost identical word, in both spelling and meaning: psyche. Look these up in a dictionary and you will see these all have to do with the mind.[10] Curiously enough, this same Greek word is sometimes translated as "mind" in the New Testament. Take for example the following verses:

---

9. *Even in the Old Testament, the word can on occasion refer to the life force. In Deuteronomy 6:5, for example, we are commanded to "love the LORD thy God with all thine heart, and with all thy soul, and with all thy might." Here, the word soul implies will power, determination, and drive. This verse is talking about serving God with all our spiritual, mental, and physical powers.*

10. *Technically, the word psyche "refers to the concept of the self, encompassing the modern ideas of soul, self, and mind." When Jesus said, "If any man will come after me, let him deny himself" he was saying we must make right choices with our mind, and not follow natural inclinations. In other words, the mind and self are closely connected concepts.*

But the unbelieving Jews stirred up the Gentiles, and made their minds evil affected against the brethren. Acts 14:2

Only let your conversation be as it becometh the gospel of Christ: that whether I come and see you, or else be absent, I may hear of your affairs, that ye stand fast in one spirit, with one mind striving together for the faith of the gospel; Philippians 1:27

For consider him that endured such contradiction of sinners against himself, lest ye be wearied and faint in your minds. Hebrews 12:3

Look up the original Greek in each of these verses, and you will see it is the exact same word translated as soul in other places: *Psuche*. We also see from these verses that the mind seems to be where choice takes place, commitment to principle, resistance to temptation. Where decisions are made. This is an important point we will come back to later.

Recognizing that the New Testament's use of the word soul is different from its use in the Old Testament helps clear up a number of verses. In Luke 2:35, for example, when the prophet Simeon told Mary "Yea, a sword shall pierce through thy own soul also," he wasn't prophesying how she would die. Rather, he was prophesying the deep inner anguish she would feel in her mind, watching that little baby she then held in her arms one day grown and hanging on a cross. Similarly, when Jesus told the parable of the rich man who pulled down his barns to build bigger ones, He describes his inner thought processes in these words: "And I will say to my soul, Soul, thou hast much goods laid up for many years; take thine ease, eat, drink, and be merry." He was talking to himself–in his mind!

And when Peter, referring to Lot, described how the inhabitants of Sodom "vexed his righteous soul from day to day with their unlawful deeds," he was not suggesting they were physically assaulting him. Rather, their lifestyles were causing him deep distress of mind!

In summary, the word soul, as it is used in the New Testament, is consistently connected with the thoughts, emotions, and choices taking place within our mind. As I've tracked down how this particular word is used–it is always connected with something conscious. It is the "self" that lives and moves around inside our skull.[11] More on this later!

It should be noted at this point, however, that this does not in any way imply a person's consciousness goes straight to heaven (or hell) at death. Despite it being a common misconception among Christians, there are at least two serious problems with this view. First, the Bible never says our "soul" goes to heaven at death. Consistently we are told it is man's "spirit" that returns to God. "Then shall the dust return to the earth as it was: and the spirit shall return unto God who gave it" (Ecclesiastes 12:7). Second, the Bible is quite clear that man's conscious thought processes come to a complete stop at death. "For the living know that they shall die: but the dead know not any thing" (Ecclesiastes 9:5). "His breath [spirit] goeth forth, he returneth to his earth [body]; in that very day his thoughts perish [the mind]" (Psalms 146:4). Nowhere in the Bible does God assign consciousness to the dead–it is instead described

---

11. *"The warfare against self is the greatest battle that was ever fought. The yielding of self, surrendering all to the will of God, requires a struggle; but the soul must submit to God before it can be renewed in holiness." Steps to Christ, p. 43.*

repeatedly as a sleep. Consciousness does not resume until the resurrection, when Christ awakens us from the slumber of the grave.[12]

THE MOST HOLY

If the Holy Place, represents the mind (soul), or the conscious thinking processes of the brain, then what would the Most Holy Place represent? What is the mysterious "spirit of man" referred to in the Bible?[13] And how is it connected to the innermost compartment of the sanctuary?

To be honest, I should have figured out what the spirit was a long time ago. The fact that it is the part of us which goes back to God at death, should have been a big clue. I guess it just never occurred to me to wonder about it. I just assumed the spirit was, well, the spirit! When I did stumble on to the answer, however, verses all over the Bible suddenly began to come alive. It started with an inspired footnote in my study Bible, commenting on I Corinthians 15, and what happens in the resurrection. Anyway, here's the quote:

---

12. The Bible points to a time when those "that sleep in the dust of the earth shall awake, some to everlasting life, and some to shame and everlasting contempt." "Marvel not at this: for the hour is coming, in the which all that are in the graves shall hear his voice, And shall come forth." John 5:28-29. This awakening takes place at the second coming of Christ. See I Thessalonians 4:13-17.

13. Some have been taught that the spirit of man is little more than life itself or some vague concept of life energy. But the Bible makes it clear man has an actual spirit. "For what man knoweth the things of a man, save the spirit of man which is in him? even so the things of God knoweth no man, but the Spirit of God." I Corinthians 2:11

*Our personal identity is preserved in the resurrection,
though not the same particles of matter or material
substance as went into the grave. The wondrous works of
God are a mystery to man. The spirit, the character of
man, is returned to God, there to be preserved. In the
resurrection every man will have his own character. God
in His own time will call forth the dead, giving again the
breath of life, and bidding the dry bones live.*[14]

Did you catch it? The spirit that returns to God is our character.
A perfect record of our character is preserved by God until the
resurrection. At that time, a new body is fashioned, the spirit or
character is restored, and instantly our thought processes
resume.[15] We wake up. One reason we have had so much
trouble trying to understand what the Bible says about
character, is simply that we have been looking up the wrong
word in our concordance!

And it makes sense to associate the Most Holy Place
with character. The most prominent feature of this compartment
was the Shekinah Glory which hovered over the mercy seat.
Glory in the Bible represents character. When Moses asked God
to show him His glory, God made all His goodness to pass
before him (Exodus 33:18-19). That is, He showed Moses His
character. Also inside the Most Holy Place was the Ark of the
Covenant which contained the two tables of stone upon which
the Law of God was inscribed. That Law is also a symbol of

---

14. *Maranatha, p. 293*

15. *This is why character change is so important in this life. At the
resurrection, the exact character we had at death is restored. If the
character has not yet been purified of sin, it would lead us to
reintroduce rebellion into the perfect environment of heaven. Our
physical bodies will be transformed when Christ returns, but the
character must be transformed here and now.*

God's character. His principles. His essence. The Most Holy Place was only entered on the Day of Atonement, a special time set aside once a year for the people to search and afflict their hearts. A time when every man's character was to be examined and evaluated before a holy God. Everything about the Most Holy Place suggests character!

And connecting the word spirit with character also makes sense. In fact, it sheds surprizing light on a number of familiar verses. Take Genesis 2:7, the verse we looked at earlier: "And the LORD God formed man of the dust of the ground, and breathed into his nostrils the breath [spirit] of life; and man became a living soul." In Hebrew (and Greek also, this time) the word for spirit and breath are identical. That is, it wasn't just air God breathed into Adam's lungs at his creation, it was spirit. His Spirit. Character. I believe it was in this sense primarily, that man was formed in the image of God. He was initially created with a character in perfect harmony with heaven.

Or take the discussion between Nicodemus and Jesus. When Jesus told the proud pharisee "Except a man be born of water and of the Spirit, he cannot enter into the kingdom of God" (John 3:5), what was He saying? Simply that without genuine character transformation, no one is going to make it! Imagine a person with a corrupt character being admitted to heaven—what would happen? The whole problem of sin would start up all over again! "That which is born of the flesh is flesh; and that which is born of the Spirit is spirit" (John 3:6). Unless there is a spiritual rebirth, a true character change, a real conversion—we are unfit for heaven.

Here's another familiar verse: "But the fruit of the Spirit is love, joy, peace, longsuffering, gentleness, goodness, faith, meekness, temperance" (Galatians 5:22-23). What is Paul saying here? Simply that when the Spirit of God comes into the life and begins to change our spirit–it produces a change in character. The terms spirit and character may not be 100% synonymous, but there is a strong overlap between them!

THE HEART OF THE MATTER

There's actually another Bible word closely connected with character: the word "heart." Frequently in Scripture, spirit and heart are used interchangeably. So whether we are talking about being "meek and lowly in heart" or about having "a meek and quiet spirit"[16], we are really talking about the same thing. Character. In fact, we still use these words exactly the same way today. We refer to someone having an angry spirit, or a kind heart–and in both cases we mean character.

Much of the Old Testament literary writings use a special form of poetry called parallelism. Basically, the writer says the same thing twice, using different but parallel words. That is, rather than rhyming sounds, like we do in most English poetry, the ancient Hebrews rhymed meanings. Which is convenient for us–because those rhymed meanings come through in the translation, whereas rhymed sounds are lost. Anyway, notice how spirit and heart are paralleled in the following verses:

> *A new heart also will I give you, and a new spirit will I put within you: and I will take away the stony heart out of your flesh, and I will give you an heart of flesh. Ezekiel 36:26*

---

16. *Matthew 11:29 and I Peter 3:4.*

*Create in me a clean heart, O God; and renew a right
spirit within me. Psalms 51:10*

*A merry heart doeth good like a medicine: but a broken
spirit drieth the bones. Proverbs 17:22*

Clearly the two words are being used interchangeably. They are
at least roughly, synonyms. And if synonyms, then both must
be connected with character.

And it is true. Just as with "spirit," once we recognize
that verses talking about the "heart" are actually talking about
character, many familiar passages begin to open up to our
understanding. Take for example these words from the lips of
Jesus about the ritualistic hand washings of His day:

*Do not ye yet understand, that whatsoever entereth in at
the mouth goeth into the belly, and is cast out into the
draught? But those things which proceed out of the mouth
come forth from the heart; and they defile the man. For
out of the heart proceed evil thoughts, murders,
adulteries, fornications, thefts, false witness,
blasphemies: These are the things which defile a man: but
to eat with unwashen hands defileth not a man.
Matthew 15:17-20*

In other words, what makes a man corrupt is character. It's
what is in the heart that counts, not what is in his stomach.
When the heart is corrupt, it leads to corrupt thoughts, and
ultimately corrupt actions. Character works its way from the
inside out.

Note that this is true on both the positive and negative
side: "A good man out of the good treasure of his heart bringeth
forth that which is good; and an evil man out of the evil treasure
of his heart bringeth forth that which is evil: for of the abundance

of the heart his mouth speaketh" (Luke 6:45). The character influences the thoughts which leads to action–in this case good or evil words. Without wanting to jump too far ahead in our study, it should begin to be clear that victory in the Christian experience is not just about controlling our actions, or even our thought-life. There must be a change in spirit, at the heart level. Real victory is the result of genuine character transformation.

It will be some time before we are ready to explore the mechanics of character development–but the importance of it is clear in this verse: "Keep thy heart with all diligence; for out of it are the issues of life" (Proverbs 4:23). Guard your character at all cost, for our choices and ultimately our actions spring out of it. Character is vital. It is at the Most Holy Place of our being. And it determines our destiny!

BEHIND THE VEIL

Think for a moment about the parallels between the divisions of the sanctuary and the regions in the nature of man. Picture that Old Testament tent. The blistering desert sand all around, the tents of Israel all in neat rows, the craggy mountains in the background. Now think: how many people could walk by and take a peek at what was happening in the Outer Court? Well, anyone. They didn't even have to be a Hebrew. The Outer Court was visible to anyone outside. In a similar way our bodies are visible to others around us. They see our form, our movements. Like the Outer Court, our external actions are open to view.

But what about inside the temple? Who could look into the Holy Place? Well, only a priest. No one else. In a similar way, no one can see into your mind–except for you. Others may guess what you are thinking, but they are limited to interpreting your physical expressions, gestures, words, etc. The actual thought processes are hidden behind closed doors.

I suspect this is what Revelation 1:6 is hinting at when it says Christ "hath made us kings and priests unto God." We are each a priest, and if a priest, there must be some temple where our service to God can be performed. An individual, personal temple. And our work as a priest must be carried out in the Holy Place of that temple. That is, in the secret place of the mind.[17] And isn't that where all real worship happens? As Mary's response to Gabriel's announcement put it: "my *soul* doth magnify the Lord" (Luke 1:46). Real worship is not just outward action–it involves even more our hidden thoughts, emotions, and choices.

Of course the most important part of the temple was the Most Holy Place. But that part was only accessible to the High Priest. Suppose you were a priest living in ancient Israel. Each day you would go into the Holy Place to perform some duty: trimming the wicks on the Golden Candlestick, replacing the cakes of bread on the Table of Shewbread, or perhaps burning some fragrance at the Altar of Incense. Each time you go in, you glance toward the veil separating you from the innermost compartment and wonder what it looks like back there. You have an idea, of course, from your study of the Scriptures: the ark, the mercy seat, the cherubim, but it is not the same. You have never *seen* it. And you can't go back and take a peek–on pain of death. To know what it really looks like, there is only one way: you must go to the High Priest and ask him!

---

17. *Perhaps this is what Jesus meant when He said, "when thou prayest, enter into thy closet, and . . . pray to thy Father which is in secret; and thy Father which seeth in secret shall reward thee openly" (Matthew 6:6). What counts is what happens in the mind.*

Seeing then that we have a great high priest, that is passed into the heavens, Jesus the Son of God, let us hold fast our profession. Hebrews 4:14.

In other words, there is a part of us that we ourselves do not fully know. We see our physical bodies. We experience the thoughts, feelings, and choices taking place in our conscious mind. But when it comes to our character–it is largely an unconscious part of our life. We don't really know ourselves.[18] We don't always know why we do what we do. The real reasons driving our choices, and ultimately our actions. But God does! To know what our character is truly like, we must go to Christ. He alone can show us our heart. He alone knows what is behind the veil.

CONCLUSION

In our study so far, we have made several critical discoveries that will be foundational to what is yet to come. First, God gave us the sanctuary to help us understand how we are made, and how to live the Spirit-filled life. And He calls our attention to it by making it clear we are each, individually, a temple. That is, the sanctuary is a blueprint or map of the moral machinery within every human being.

Second, the basic floor plan of the building parallels nicely the basic partitions in the nature of man. The Outer Court matches our outward physical body, and the actions of our body. The inner man is divided into two distinct parts: our conscious mind or soul (*Psuche*) and a deeper heart or spirit,

---

18. *Note the question God raises in the book of Jeremiah, and His answer: "The heart is deceitful above all things . . .who can know it? I the LORD search the heart." Jeremiah 17:9-10.*

hidden behind the veil. The first refers to the thoughts, emotions, and choices that constantly run through our head. The self. The latter, refers to our character, of which we are largely unconscious. To know the truth about what really drives us, we must go to our High Priest: Jesus Christ.

We've also hinted that true victory is more than outward compliance to a list of prescribed actions. And it is even more than rigidly trying to control our thought life. It involves a change of character, for it is this character that prompts our thoughts and ultimately our actions–to either good or evil. True victory involves developing a character that consistently prompts us in the right direction, and then instantly responding to those promptings. To understand how one obtains this kind of victory will be the goal of the chapters ahead.

Before we can get there however, we need to fill in more pieces of this sketchy map we have been drawing of the moral machinery. In particular, we must turn our attention to the pieces of furniture connected with the sanctuary and the various faculties each one represents. Keep reading–things are about to get even more amazing.

Review Questions
Chapter 2–First Principles

1.	How many divisions were there in the sanctuary? How does this parallel how God has made man.

2.	In what ways does the Outer Court represent our physical body?

3.	Explain what the word "soul" means in the New Testament? How does it fit into the sanctuary?

4.	What part of the sanctuary corresponds to the "spirit" of man? Explain what the spirit is in your own words.

5.	What is the significance of the fact only the High Priest could go into the Most Holy Place? How is that important to you?

Battle for the Mind
Chapter 3

This I say then, Walk in the Spirit, and ye shall not
fulfil the lust of the flesh. For the flesh lusteth
against the Spirit, and the Spirit against the flesh:
and these are contrary the one to the other:
so that ye cannot do the things that ye would.
Galatians 5:16-17

My wife does a wonderful job of making our house look like a home–with all those little knick-knacks, house plants, family pictures, and the like that make it feel special. But there's one downside to her creativity. Every few months she will get inspired with the thought of rearranging our furniture. Once I see that light in her eyes, I know the outcome. The next free day or two is going to be devoted to moving things around. There's no way around it!

The trouble is trying to get around the rearranged bookshelves, tables, and couches at night. Until I get used to their new locations I forget where things are and usually end up stubbing my toe or tripping over something because it is not where I remembered. Eventually I get used to the change, but until then I've got a good chance of knocking something over on the way to my destination.

Much of the confusion we experience in regards to the moral machinery inside us is not so different. We have some sense of the various moral faculties within man–but we don't really understand where they are positioned, or how they interrelate. And as a result, life is like walking through an unfamiliar house with a blindfold. Mapping out the furniture in the sanctuary can help. By linking each faculty to a specific piece of furniture, we can determine their precise locations, and gain valuable insights into how they function.

ALTAR OF BURNT SACRIFICE

The first faculty we will study is what the Bible calls the "flesh." It is that part of us which is constantly pulling us to make choices contrary to the will of God. "For the flesh lusteth against the Spirit, and the Spirit against the flesh: and these are contrary the one to the other: so that ye cannot do the things that ye would" (Galatians 5:17). "So then they that are in the flesh cannot please God" (Romans 8:8). It consists of our physical cravings, lusts, and drives. It seems to be connected with what is called our limbic system–the chemical responses in our body that cause us to feel anger, sexual desire, appetite, and the like.[19] Originally these drives were all in perfect harmony with the Law of God, but at man's fall, they became corrupted, and now tend to draw us away from God.[20] They are "not subject to the law of God, neither indeed can be" (Romans 8:7).

---

19. In Galatians 5:24, we read that the flesh consists of "affections and lusts." The Greek words used here suggest physical pains, passions, longings, appetites and desires.

20. Even today, our physical drives are important. They remind us of our need for food, water, and rest. These drives become distorted, however, when there is imbalance or excess.

Paul makes it clear these drives are rooted in our body: "For I know that in me (that is, in my flesh,) dwelleth no good thing: for to will is present with me; but how to perform that which is good I find not" (Romans 7:18). A few verses later he again connects them with our physical body–the Outer Court, so to speak: "For I delight in the law of God after the inward man: but I see another law in my members, warring against the law of my mind, and bringing me into captivity to the law of sin which is in my members . . . who shall deliver me from the body of this death?" (Romans 7:22-24). We cannot discuss everything referred to in this passage at this time, but one thing is clear: the problem of the flesh is somehow embedded in our body.[21] And it is passed down from one generation to the next–almost as if it were encoded right into the DNA of our cells. In fact, the New Testament uses the exact same Greek word (*Sarx*) to refer to both the flesh and the body. Clearly the two are connected.

Was there a piece of furniture in the Outer Court that somehow parallels this faculty? There was, in fact, only one place in the sanctuary involving "flesh" and it was the outermost Altar of Burnt Sacrifice. It is also the place where animals were put to death–which reminds us what must happen to the flesh nature: "they that are Christ's have crucified the flesh with the affections and lusts" (Galatians 5:24). We will discuss how this is done shortly.

---

21. *"The lower passions have their seat in the body and work through it. The words 'flesh' or 'fleshly' or 'carnal lusts' embrace the lower, corrupt nature; the flesh of itself cannot act contrary to the will of God. We are commanded to crucify the flesh, with the affections and lusts. How shall we do it? Shall we inflict pain on the body? No; but put to death the temptation to sin. The corrupt thought is to be expelled. Every thought is to be brought into captivity to Jesus Christ." Reflecting Christ, p. 144.*

It should be noted that while we can live in such a way that the flesh has no power to control our choices–it remains a part of our experience until our bodies are transformed. This is confusing to many new Christians–who assume their sinful cravings will disappear at conversion. Conversion implants new spiritual desires in our spirit, but the flesh continues to clamor until the second coming of Christ, when our body is changed.

> *In a moment, in the twinkling of an eye . . . the dead shall be raised incorruptible, and we shall be changed. For this corruptible must put on incorruption, and this mortal must put on immortality. I Corinthians 15:52-53*

Until that moment, we must wage a constant battle against "fleshly lusts, which war against the soul" (I Peter 2:11) anticipating the day when Christ "shall change our vile body, that it may be fashioned like unto his glorious body" (Philippians 3:20-21). A exciting new body, free from even the desire for sin!

THE BRASS LAVER

In the Outer Court, there was a second piece of furniture just beyond the Altar of Burnt Sacrifice. It was called the Laver, and was essentially a large basin of water used by the priests to wash their hands and feet. This Laver seems to be a symbol of another important faculty of the body: action.

The act of washing should immediately bring to mind the ceremony of baptism, where our past sins (wrong actions) are washed away.[22] It also brings to mind the time Jesus washed

---

22. See Acts 22:16.

the feet of His disciples. There, Jesus explained that it was a lesser cleansing, to wash away any wrong acts committed since their baptism. "He that is washed [baptism] needeth not save to wash his feet, but is clean every whit" (John 13:10). Washing the hands, like washing the feet, also seems to point to action: "Whatsoever thy hand findeth to do, do it with all thy might" (Ecclesiastes 9:10).

When the laver was originally made, it was constructed of brass from "the lookingglasses of the women assembling, which assembled at the door of the tabernacle" (Exodus 38:8). This reminds us that there is a place for self-reflection on our actions. "Examine yourselves, whether ye be in the faith; prove your own selves" (II Corinthians 13:5). While we may not know all that is in the heart, we can certainly see our outward acts. We are to be "like unto a man beholding his natural face in a glass," looking "into the perfect law of liberty" that we may be "a doer of the work" (James 1:23,25). That is, every action is to be in harmony with the moral law. "For by the law is the knowledge of sin" (Romans 3:20). "Whosoever committeth sin transgresseth also the law: for sin is the transgression of the law" (I John 3:4).

The Laver is an important reminder that the body is not inherently evil. True, it is corrupted by sinful cravings, and those cravings have to be put to death–but the body itself is a gift from God, "fearfully and wonderfully made" (Psalms 139:14). It is the only instrument available to us for serving God and man in this world, and as such should be valued and preserved in the best possible condition. In times past, some Christians believed it was necessary to inflict severe punishment on the physical body. A more biblical attitude is to "glorify God in your body" by wisely caring for its needs

(I Corinthians 6:20). As Paul noted, "every man that striveth for the mastery is temperate in all things. Now they do it to obtain a corruptible crown; but we an incorruptible. I therefore . . . keep under my body, and bring it into subjection" (I Corinthians 9:25-27). The Laver, thus, challenges us to preserve our physical powers to the fullest extent possible, that we may render a more vigorous life of obedience to God.[23] With every action pure and undefiled. Washed and clean.

CURTAINS AND PILLARS

Before moving from the Outer Court into the Holy Place, it is worth pausing a moment at the door. According to the Bible, the door was a hanging of "blue, and purple, and scarlet" suspended from five pillars positioned at the front of the building.[24] That is, to go from the body to the mind, one must pass through these five pillars. What might they represent? It may be coincidence, but I believe God was hinting here at our physical senses: sight, sound, taste, touch, and smell. Or to put it differently, these senses are the avenues to the mind. To protect our soul from contamination, we must be careful to guard these avenues. What we watch. What we listen to. The senses are the chief means through which sin enters and pollutes the sanctuary.

---

23. The importance of maintaining peak physical health is evident in this prayer of the Apostle John: "I wish above all things that thou mayest prosper and be in health, even as thy soul prospereth." See III John 1:2. Clearly, health is an important part of sanctification.

24. Exodus 26:36-37

Curiously, the veil between the Holy Place and the Most Holy Place was a curtain made of similar kinds of materials, but it was suspended from four pillars instead of five.[25] I believe these represent our spiritual senses. The Bible identifies certain faculties as being directly connected with the heart or spirit. And like our physical senses, these communicate information to our conscious mind–but in the form of "impressions" or "promptings." Or to put it differently, these senses tap into the spiritual realm, rather than the physical realm. They are communications transmitted from behind the veil. We will be studying these faculties in much more detail in a future chapter. For now, I just wish to mention that in my study of the Bible, there appear to be exactly four spiritual senses, matching the number of pillars in the veil exactly. Again, it may be coincidence, but I don't think so.

THE ARK OF THE COVENANT

In order to understand how the various compartments of the sanctuary building relate to each other, it will be helpful to identify at least one of the faculties connected with the Most Holy Place. All four function in similar ways, but for simplicity's sake, I will focus on the one people seem to grasp most intuitively. That faculty we turn to now is called the conscience. We will explore the others more fully in chapter six.

Like all the spiritual senses, the Bible directly connects the faculty of conscience with the Most Holy Place. Take a moment, for example, to unpack the following verses:

---

25. *Exodus 26:31-33*

For when the Gentiles, which have not the law, do by nature the things contained in the law, these, having not the law, are a law unto themselves: Which shew the work of the law written in their hearts, their conscience also bearing witness, and their thoughts the mean while accusing or else excusing one another; Romans 2:14-15

Paul seems to be saying that even among groups with no access to the Scriptures, there are individuals who do things in harmony with the law: they are honest, faithful to their spouse, show respect to authority, don't kill or steal, etc. The existence of these individuals has a convicting influence on others in the group, because there is something in the heart of man that is drawn toward righteousness. That faculty is called the conscience–and it sends back either "accusing" or "excusing" messages from the heart to the mind. We tend to be more familiar with the accusing messages, but the excusing messages are also important. They give us confidence our course is right, when faced with opposition or potential loss. Both are needed!

Notice that the conscience is rooted in the law of God, which is written in the heart of man. In the Old Testament, the Ten Commandments were kept in the Ark of the Covenant, in the Most Holy Place. Despite the fact sin may be engraved on our personal "tables of stone," our spiritual natures were designed to operate in harmony with heaven.[26] That is, there is a part of us that responds to the moral law. This sensitivity to

---

26. *The Bible frequently talks about the tables of the heart, which may be thought of as a record or transcript of our character, the principles we live by. In Jeremiah 17:1, an example is given of individuals who have sin written into their character. In II Corinthians 3:3, we find characters in harmony with heaven. Notice the sanctuary language in both verses.*

right and wrong, is like a spiritual sense.[27] Basically, the conscience discerns spiritual information from behind the veil and sends that information to the conscious mind in the form of impressions. It is closely connected with the convicting power of the Holy Spirit.

Paul describes this process in several places. For example, "I say the truth in Christ, I lie not, my conscience also bearing me witness in the Holy Ghost" (Romans 9:1). Note the close connection between the conscience and the Holy Spirit, which once again points back to the Most Holy Place, where the Spirit of God was manifest in the Shekinah Glory.[28] Yet the conscience is also bearing witness to Paul's conscious mind. Communication was taking place from the spirit to the mind, about information in the spiritual realm, much as our physical senses involve communication between the body and the mind about what is happening in the physical world around us. To put it differently, the mind is positioned directly in the middle between the promptings of our flesh, and the promptings of the Spirit.

THE BATTLEFIELD

Which means the mind is the battlefield. On the one hand, the enemy uses various things in the world to stir up

---

27. Here is how one writer describes it: "The eye is the sensitive conscience, the inner light of the mind. Upon its correct view of things the spiritual healthfulness of the whole soul and being depend." The passage goes on to explain how the Word of God, "makes the conscience smart under its application" but brings healing to the life. Our High Calling, p.350.

28. All our spiritual faculties respond to the movings of the Holy Spirit. God's Spirit speaks to our spirit in the form of promptings or impressions. This is the essence of spiritual discernment.

desires in our flesh that cannot be fulfilled without violating the Law of God. And on the other, God is trying to send messages to our mind through our spiritual faculties, such as the conscience, to act in harmony with His will. Caught in the middle is the mind—which must decide which promptings it will follow. This is the crux of the matter.

Note how Paul describes it: "For the flesh lusteth against the Spirit, and the Spirit against the flesh: and these are contrary the one to the other" (Galatians 5:17). Which promptings we yield to, determines whether we are fleshly or spiritual. "For they that are after the flesh do mind the things of the flesh; but they that are after the Spirit the things of the Spirit. For to be carnally minded is death; but to be spiritually minded is life and peace." (Romans 8:5-6). The day to day battles we face are largely a struggle over which impulses we will submit to: the spirit or the flesh.

In order to understand this battle, we must turn at last to the furniture in the Holy Place. In our study so far, we've noticed three particular faculties repeatedly connected with the mind: reason, the emotions, and will. Not surprisingly, there are three pieces of furniture in this compartment of the sanctuary. Learning to use these faculties as God intended is essentially to have the mind of Christ. And there is no other path to victory. Or as Peter put it, "arm yourselves likewise with the same mind" for he who has done this "hath ceased from sin" (I Peter 4:1).

THE TABLE OF SHEWBREAD

Let's start with the Table of Shewbread. This piece of furniture was used to display two stacks of cakes, called the bread of His presence, with six cakes in each stack. In the

Bible, bread is often used as a symbol for the Word of God. In the wilderness temptation, for example, Jesus said "Man shall not live by bread alone, but by every word that proceedeth out of the mouth of God" (Matthew 4:4). After feeding the 5000, Jesus said "if any man eat of this bread, he shall live for ever" and then made it clear He was really talking about his words (John 6:51, 63). This is where our reasoning powers should focus–on Scripture. "This book of the law shall not depart out of thy mouth; but thou shalt meditate therein day and night" (Joshua 1:8). Meditation involves reason, logic and analysis.

The two stacks of cakes also help us to understand the proper function of reason. Not only do they point to the Bible, but they also hint at a balance or scale. Six and six–the two stacks were always evenly matched. Which implies reason's primary purpose is simply to evaluate whether or not something matches up with Scripture. Not every impression is from God. How we were raised, past experiences, education, and even our cultivated quirks of personality, all come into play. The flesh is always around. And in fact, the enemy seems able to implant impressions as well.[29] For this reason, it is vital that we "believe not every spirit, but try the spirits whether they are of God" (I John 4:1). To properly strengthen our reasoning powers is to increase our ability to understand and interpret Scripture correctly.

In order for reason to function properly, however, it must be kept under strict obedience to Christ.[30] Otherwise, the

---

29. When Peter rebuked Jesus for prophesying His death, Jesus recognized it was Satan prompting Peter to oppose the will of God. Jesus "turned, and said unto Peter, Get thee behind me, Satan." Matthew 16:23.

30. See II Corinthians 10:4-5.

tendency of fallen human nature is to drift toward *rationalization*. That is, we justify or make excuses for wrong choices. At some point along the way, it occurred to me that rationalizations are ultimately a failure of reason to ask the right question. When we say some act is just a small thing–we're asking how big it is, rather than whether or not it is biblical. When we say others are doing it, so it must be ok–we're asking how others view that action, and not how the Bible views it. When we convince ourselves some choice is too hard, or the consequences too great–we're asking if the choice is going to be easy, instead of if it is in harmony with Scripture. When we tell ourselves it is the motive that counts, or that the end justifies the means–we are sidestepping the real issue of whether or not the decision lines up with God's Word. To avoid rationalization we must discipline our mind to ask the critical question. What does the Bible really say?

THE GOLDEN CANDLESTICK

The Candlestick is not much harder to identify, thanks to more helpful clues. In the Sermon on the Mount, we read "Let your light so shine before men, that they may see your good works, and glorify your Father which is in heaven" (Matthew 5:16). The word "let" implies choice. Our life gives light, when we choose to live in such a way that God is glorified. Similarly, we read in the book of Hebrews this description of Jesus: "Thou hast loved righteousness, and hated iniquity; therefore God, even thy God, hath anointed thee with the oil of gladness above thy fellows" (Hebrews 1:9). In other words, the "oil" mentioned in this verse was given because

Jesus consistently chose to do right.[31] Oil, of course, was the fuel powering the flames of the Candlestick. The Candlestick, thus seems to represent the will. In the words of Joshua, it symbolizes a call to "choose you this day whom ye will serve" (Joshua 24:15). Choose Christ and we "shall not walk in darkness, but shall have the light of life" (John 8:12).

It is a fitting symbol in many ways. The seven branches of the Candlestick remind us we are to live for Christ seven days a week. Not just on our weekly day of worship–but in the classroom, our workplace, our homes. We must be continually choosing Christ. Each morning and evening the priests would go into the temple and trim away the blackened, charred wicks, then refill the Candlestick with fresh supplies of oil. This is a beautiful picture of our daily need to confess our sin before God, and cut it out of our life. And also of our need to recommit ourselves to God, that we might be filled with "fresh supplies" of the Holy Spirit. It is only through daily confession, and personal consecration that we can keep our lives burning bright in the darkness around us.

As with reason, for the will to function properly it must be empowered by grace. Most Christians know by experience that trying to continually choose right in our own strength is an exercise in futility and frustration.[32] Unfortunately, believers

---

31. According to Acts 5:32, "the Holy Ghost" is "given to them that obey [God]." If we want more of the Spirit in our life, we too must choose righteousness, and reject iniquity. We cannot have spiritual power without making right choices.

32. According to Jeremiah 13:23, those who are used to doing evil can no more do good than leopards can change the pattern of their spots, or Ethiopians the color of their skin. As one writer put it, "Your promises and resolutions are like ropes of sand." Steps to Christ, p. 47.

sometimes fall into the other ditch of expecting God to give us total victory without any effort on our part. Some seem to think of surrender as an entirely passive process, where God holds all the strings and we dangle about with no more initiative than a marionette. But this is not a healthy view of the will, either. Marionettes do not experience growth in character, for growth requires decision-making. No, victory comes through the right *action* of the will.

It took me quite a while to discover how the will is supposed to work. While struggling to find a clearer understanding of how divinity and humanity work together, I stumbled across this amazing quotation:

> *God does not design that our will should be destroyed, for it is only through its exercise that we can accomplish what He would have us do. Our will is to be yielded to Him, that we may receive it again, purified and refined, and so linked in sympathy with the Divine that He can pour through us the tides of His love and power.*[33]

There's the balance! We must indeed surrender the will to God. But then we must also understand that God promptly returns our will to us, miraculously transformed and energized in such a way that it is now capable of issuing commands that will be carried out by the body. Yet it is the human will that issues those commands![34]

---

33. *Thoughts from the Mount of Blessings, p. 62.*

34. *"In the work of redemption there is no compulsion. No external force is employed. Under the influence of the Spirit of God, man is left free to choose whom he will serve. In the change that takes place when the soul surrenders to Christ, there is the highest sense of freedom. The expulsion of sin is the act of the soul itself. True, we*

Paul clearly recognized, that it was God's grace that gave him success in his life and ministry. But he also recognized that grace was activated through human choice. "But by the grace of God I am what I am: and his grace which was bestowed upon me was not in vain; but I laboured more abundantly than they all" (I Corinthians 15:10). "Whereunto I also labour, striving according to his working, which worketh in me mightily" (Colossians 1:29). This is why Paul encouraged believers to "work out your own salvation with fear and trembling" while simultaneously acknowledging "it is God which worketh in you" (Philippians 2:12-13). For the will to function properly there must be a blending of human exertion with a dependency on divine power. We will explore this topic more fully in our next chapter.

THE ALTAR OF INCENSE

Which leaves one last piece of furniture to represent the emotions: the Altar of Incense. And again, several interesting parallels come to mind. For example, we are described as "a sweet savour of Christ" in II Corinthians 2:15. That savour is largely manifest through the emotions evident in our life: love, joy, peace, and the rest. It is this fragrance that attracts people to Christ. In contrast, those filled with fear, anger, or despair exude a very different kind of aroma. Strong emotions are even described a bit like incense in the Bible: "therefore was the king very wroth, and his anger burned in him" (Esther 1:12). Notice

---

have no power to free ourselves from Satan's control; but when we desire to be set free from sin, and in our great need cry out for a power out of and above ourselves, the powers of the soul are imbued with the divine energy of the Holy Spirit, and they obey the dictates of the will in fulfilling the will of God." Desire of Ages, p. 466.

the language here is not so different from that used today. Incense is also connected with prayer: "Let my prayer be set forth before thee as incense" (Psalms 141:2).[35] And of course, that is what we are to do with both good and bad emotions: bring them to God in prayer. Rather than voicing frustrations, disappointments, and hurts to our fellow man, we can pour out our feelings to God in the secret place of prayer and receive courage, comfort, and strength. Hopes and joys are to be expressed in worship and vibrant praise.

In the minds of many Christians, emotions are viewed in a negative light, in contrast to reason which is viewed as something more positive. However, unsanctified reason is no more reliable than unsanctified emotion. In the book of Proverbs we read, "trust in the LORD with all thine heart; and lean not unto thine own understanding" (Proverbs 3:5). And again, "there is a way which seemeth right unto a man, but the end thereof are the ways of death" (Proverbs 14:12). In the New Testament, Paul says something similar: "For the wisdom of this world is foolishness with God" (I Corinthians 3:19). And conversely, "the world by wisdom knew not God"–to them, the cross is "foolishness" (I Corinthians 1:21, 18). Rather, it is the misuse of emotion and reason (and for that matter, the will), that we should guard against.

The fact is, God created emotions. God intended Adam and Eve to experience the emotional joys of a beautiful sunset, the singing of birds, love for one another, and the worship of God. Jesus frequently experienced strong emotions including

---

35. *The life of discipleship can be captured in the Holy Place, prayer at the Altar of Incense, Bible study at the Table of Shewbread and obedience at the Golden Candlestick. Furthermore, the importance of witnessing can be seen in our role as priests of God.*

compassion, sorrow, indignation, and anguish.[36] When humans attempt to shut down their emotional sensitivities, they miss out on much of the fullness of life: the enjoyment of simple pleasures, friendship and love, the satisfaction of accomplishment, and much more. Worship loses its authenticity and degenerates into rote formalism. We also begin to lose our ability to empathize with people, and can miss subtle signals they are communicating. My wife and daughter both tend to be more connected emotionally than I am, and they frequently "sense" things about people I completely miss. That kind of discernment is a great gift.

I believe God created our emotions to serve as a kind of early warning detection system. Have you ever listened to some speaker and felt something was not quite right with their message? You couldn't pinpoint the error, but something troubled you. Or you found yourself in a situation where you didn't quite feel safe. You looked around and couldn't identify any specific threats, but you sensed danger just the same. Or maybe you were offered a seemingly exciting opportunity, but something just felt fishy. All of these are signals that come to us through the emotions. Many times, our emotions pick up on things intuitively, much faster than reason. It is akin to smelling smoke before you see the flame. Or in this case, smelling the incense. We ignore these warnings at our peril!

The problem arises when we use the emotions as a guidance system rather than a detection system. The emotions pick up a wide range of signals, but they are not well equipped to filter the information. That role is delegated to reason. Allowing emotions to direct our choices, leads to an up and

---

36. For examples, see Matthew 9:36, John 11:35, John 2:13-17, Luke 22:44.

down roller coaster kind of experience. Emotions are often fickle and inconsistent, and can lead to rash and impulsive decisions. Probably all of us have acted on some fleeting impression without thinking first, and know by experience how much trouble that can get us into! The goal is not to shut down the emotions—we need sensitivity and discernment. But we must remember their purpose: detection, not direction.

THE MYSTERIOUS BRIDGE

The Altar of Incense is a particularly interesting piece of furniture—as it seems to be something of a bridge between the Holy Place and the Most Holy Place. For one thing, of all the furniture in the Holy Place, it was closest to the Most Holy Place. Another link is the fact that the incense from this piece of furniture filled both chambers of the sanctuary building. Neither light from the Candlestick, nor bread from the Table went behind the veil—but the smoke was able to filter through the curtain, thus connecting both compartments. In fact, for reasons I do not fully understand other than perhaps to make this point exactly, the writer of Hebrews connects the golden censer (which was part of the Altar of Incense) with the innermost compartment. See Hebrews 9:3-5.[37]

This bridge makes sense, of course. The emotions in many ways are closely connected to character. A person filled with the Spirit of God, and a character in harmony with heaven, will feel love, joy, and peace. Specific emotions. In a similar way, when a person's character has been scarred by ridicule,

---

37. Technically, Hebrews is correct. The censer was used on the Day of Atonement to carry incense from the Altar of Incense back behind the veil into the Most Holy Place.

abuse, guilt or bitterness, that individual will struggle with persistent negative emotions.[38] Reason can be directed, and the will disciplined, but our emotions come largely unbidden. They are something like a foggy window, allowing a partial glimpse into the heart. Interestingly, in English we often assign the word "heart" both these shades of meaning. We describe someone as having a heavy heart (emotion) or remark how kind-hearted they are (character)–recognizing intuitively that the Altar of Incense and the Most Holy Place are somehow connected. Understanding this bridge is important in helping us to grasp how God works in a person's life.

HOW GOD WORKS

This introductory survey of the furniture in the sanctuary prepares us to understand the process by which God attempts to transform the life. It begins with an impression from the Holy Spirit. God sends hundreds of them every day–perhaps thousands. Constantly trying to nudge us in the right direction. God may use any of the four spiritual faculties, but they are all closely related and work the same way. For the sake of illustration, let's suppose it is the conscience. Like a physical sense organ, the conscience receives these spiritual messages and then attempts to communicate that information to the mind.

Where in the Holy Place is that witness of the conscience first detected? We've already seen the close link between the Altar of Incense and the Most Holy Place. It shouldn't surprise us that the Bible clearly implicates the emotions in this role.

---

38. *Even negative emotions play an important role in our life, for they call attention to problems in the character, hidden behind the veil. We will discuss how to deal with these in a future chapter.*

Accusing messages from the conscience are registered as the emotion of guilt or sorrow for sin: "My sorrow is continually before me. For I will declare mine iniquity; I will be sorry for my sin" (Psalms 38:17-18). The excusing messages of the conscience, those affirming our course is right, are registered as joy: "For our rejoicing is this, the testimony of our conscience" (II Corinthians 1:12). In this verse, the testimony of his conscience–that his life was pleasing to God–produced the wonderful emotion of joy. Anyone who has ever cleared a guilty conscience by confessing some sin or righting some wrong knows the dramatic change in emotions that can occur.

In other words, spiritual promptings generally come to us in the form of an impression or feeling through our emotions–and less often as direct words or thoughts. We say our spirit is "troubled" (Psalms 77:3). Like thousands on the day of Pentecost, we are "pricked in [our] heart" (Acts 2:37). Or on the flip side–we sense a peace from God that our course is right.[39] We have an assurance or conviction, an "unction" from the Holy Spirit (I John 2:20). If everything is working as it should, the emotion will quickly detect these promptings. We catch the scent of the burning incense.

Next, the impression is sent over to reason for evaluation. The heart can be deceitful, remember, and it generally contains a mixture of biblical and non-biblical principles. So it is vital that each prompting be tested against Scripture. If our reasoning powers are under the control of Christ, they will focus on one question: is this impulse in

---

39. In Colossians 3:15, Paul says, "let the peace of God rule in your hearts." The word translated "rule" in this verse means to judge, referee, or arbitrate. That is, the feeling of God's peace can be a help to us in discerning God's will.

harmony with the Word of God? And we will stedfastly resist any tendency toward rationalization. As honestly and as accurately as possible, we set the impression on one side of the Table of Shewbread, and the Bible on the other—and then check to see if the two measure up evenly.

Once reason is able to discern that an impression is indeed in harmony with the Word of God, it is sent over to the will for execution. Without divine power, we frequently find ourselves incapable of carrying out the actions that reason knows are in our own best interest. But when we cry out to God for strength, the will can be empowered with divine energy and issue a command to the body that will be obeyed. The key is to consecrate ourselves to God, and receive an infilling of the Holy Spirit. Oil for the flame. Then we engage the will. We choose to act. Without the infusion of divine power, our will is powerless. With it, the will is omnipotent.

Emotion detects. Reason evaluates. The will executes. Of course, the will cannot actually carry out any action—it simply issues the command to the body to act on the impression. Which brings us to the final step in the process: action. When all these pieces of furniture are working properly, an impression can pass through these faculties in a matter of seconds, producing almost instantaneous obedience. When that happens consistently, the cravings of the flesh are rendered powerless, and we experience a life of victory. This is what it means to crucify the flesh—to consistently follow the promptings of the Spirit instead. It is what makes our life a witness to the world.

Review again the steps involved, visualizing the prompting as it passes through each piece of furniture in the sanctuary:

God sends a message through the Spirit.
The conscience receives it, and pricks the mind.
The emotions detect the prompting.
Reason verifies it is from God using Scripture.
The will issues a command to act.
The body responds with an act of obedience.
The flesh is crucified on that specific point.

As Christians, it is vital that we learn how each piece of the moral machinery works, and then cooperate with God in using them rightly. That is, we need the mind of Christ.

THE ENEMY'S STRATEGY

Unfortunately, there are multiple points along this path where the process can break down. And the enemy has set snares at every piece of furniture in the sanctuary in hopes of making us stumble. We have addressed some of those attacks already in this chapter. But let's take a moment to consider his overarching strategy. In short, while God works from the inside out, Satan tries to work from the outside in.

God's process ends with our life being a consistent witness to the world around us. Satan's strategy begins by using the world to entice us toward evil. According to I John 5:19, "the whole world lieth in wickedness." That is, because of sin, the pervasive influence of the world is contrary to God. There is certainly beauty and good in the world around us, but by and large, the world now walks "according to the prince of the power of the air, the spirit that now worketh in the children of disobedience" (Ephesians 2:2). One doesn't need much exposure to secular media to see its value system is out of step with the Bible. Christians use the term "worldliness" to describe this persistent pull in the wrong direction exerted through our culture, society, and environment. Paul warns us of it in these words: "be not conformed to this world: but be ye transformed by the renewing of your mind" (Romans 12:2). Similarly, Jesus said, "I pray not that thou shouldest take them out of the world, but that thou shouldest keep them from the evil" (John 17:15).

The world appeals primarily to the flesh. That is, it stirs up passions, lusts, and appetites in the body that cannot be fulfilled in a moral way. It attracts us to do things that are contrary to God–and the body awakens to those attractions. Imagine a piece of chocolate cake. Luscious, moist, and sweet. You see its rich color and texture. Your nose whiffs the sweet, earthy fragrance. Your mouth begins to water. The body responds, and you reach for a piece. It goes from the Altar of Burnt Sacrifice, to the Laver.

Notice how the senses were involved. The five pillars between the Outer Court and the Holy Place. Temptation comes to the mind from the flesh, through the senses. Guarding the avenues to the soul is one defense. We are to "make no provision for the flesh, to fulfil the lusts thereof" (Romans 14:12). But as long as we live in this world–it will be impossible to shut out all sources of temptation.[40] And the enemy knows this. Therefore it is critical that we learn to resist.

The part of the mind Satan targets first is the will. His goal is not primarily to convince you logically that eating chocolate cake is good for you, or that it will make you emotionally joyous–rather it is simply to get you to give in. Just this once. It will be delicious. Go for it! How many times have

---

40. Paul said we cannot completely escape exposure to the world, "for then must ye needs go out of the world. also." I Corinthians 5:9-10

you heard those subtle whispers? Unless we learn to engage the will in full reliance on the power of God, our powers of resistance are minimal. It may not happen every time, or in every situation, but he will eventually get us. We will yield the will and come under his power.[41]

Once the will is taken—Satan next targets our reasoning powers. We begin to justify our wrong action. We find rationalizations for our choice, and if we can't think of any, he's happy to suggest some of his own! This is the process by which man becomes self-deceived.[42] Rather than simply confessing our sin, and repenting before God, pride kicks in. We convince our self it wasn't really bad. Everyone does it. It was just a small piece. You only do it every once in a while. Slowly we persuade ourselves, and eventually we come to believe wrong is right. Reason fails.

After reason is conquered, Satan proceeds to attack the emotions. During the whole time Satan was busy tempting us to do wrong, God was sending spiritual promptings to do right. Promptings picked up by our emotional sensitivities. There were two voices, in other words, advocating both good and evil within our mind. Once reason becomes convinced the wrong course is right, however, it begins to resist and reject the opposing messages. The mind starts to tune out those nagging

---

41. *"Know ye not, that to whom ye yield yourselves servants to obey, his servants ye are to whom ye obey; whether of sin unto death, or of obedience unto righteousness?" Romans 6:16. We come under the power of the one we submit to.*

42. *Jesus said, "If any man will do his will, he shall know of the doctrine." John 7:17. Similarly, James wrote, "be ye doers of the word, and not hearers only, deceiving your own selves." James 1:22. Our ability to receive truth is determined more by our willingness to obey God, than any intellectual or educational advantages we may have.*

feelings, and gradually succeeds in silencing them. This is one reason that giving in to temptation is so dangerous. It eventually dulls our ability to detect future promptings from the Spirit of God in a particular area.

Which is Satan's real objective–to sever our connection with God. In this case, by disabling the faculty of conscience. With each violation, the conscience becomes defiled. See I Corinthians 8:7. By the time some emotional sensitivity is silenced, the conscience is "seared" as "with a hot iron" (I Timothy 4:2). When all sensitivity is lost–our connection with God is fully severed, and there is little more He can do. In shutting down the voice of conscience (or any of our other spiritual faculties), Satan shuts down the means God uses to communicate with our mind. And he triumphs.

SUMMARY

So God works from the inside out: the Spirit speaks to the conscience, emotions pick up the message, reason verifies its authenticity, the will issues the command, and the body acts–crucifying the flesh. Ultimately, God's will is for us to become a witness to the world through our obedience on that point. Satan uses the world to appeal to our flesh, largely through our senses, to overpower the will, compromise our reason, and shut down our emotional sensitivities. His goal is to defile the conscience, and ultimately sever our connection with God. It is a constant battle waged hundreds of times each day. A battle fought within the mind. Every decision makes our mind that much more spiritual, or that much more fleshly. Over time, a man is either ennobled or degraded. And in the process, our character is shaped and our destiny determined.

Before we can look more fully at what the Bible teaches about character, however, we must pause a moment to look at the secret to winning these inner battles consistently. The secret to continual power from God. The secret to victory. It is a vitally important topic. Keep reading. . .

Review Questions
Chapter 3–Battle for the Mind

1. List the furniture in the Outer Court, and identify the faculties they represent.

2. What pieces of furniture were in the Holy Place? What do they symbolize?

3. Give an example of a spiritual faculty, and how it is linked to the Ark of the Covenant in the Most Holy Place.

4. How were the five pillars of the door important? What about the four pillars of the veil? Explain.

5. Contrast God's plan to transform the life with Satan's strategy to destroy us. Trace these processes through the sanctuary.

Power for Victory
Chapter 4

For I am not ashamed of the gospel of Christ:
for it is the power of God unto salvation
to every one that believeth; to the Jew first,
and also to the Greek. For therein is the
righteousness of God revealed from faith to faith:
as it is written, The just shall live by faith.
Romans 1:16-17

So far we have seen how the sanctuary is a powerful model of man's moral machinery. A map, or blueprint, of how God has made us. Not only does it describe the basic regions within man (the body, mind, and spirit), but it gives powerful insights into the various faculties located within each region. The body is afflicted with a measure of corruption, called the flesh. It also is blessed with the faculty of action. The mind has three primary faculties: the emotions, reason, and will. Combined, they form conscious thought. Finally, the spirit or heart of man is the location of character. It is also the base of various spiritual faculties, of which we have briefly explored only one: the conscience. Each of these faculties can be directly connected with one or another of the various pieces of furniture in the sanctuary.

We have also gained some insight into how they interrelate. The spirit and flesh are in constant conflict. God prompts our mind through our spirit to move in harmony with His will as revealed in the Word. Satan uses the world to draw our mind toward his will, through the flesh. One set of promptings are communicated through our spiritual senses. The other through our physical senses. The physical senses, can be represented by the five pillars upholding the curtain separating the Outer Court from the Holy Place: sight, sound, taste, touch and smell. And the spiritual senses can be represented by the four pillars upholding the veil between the Holy Place and the Most Holy Place. This places the mind at the center of the battle between right and wrong that rages every day in our life.

The question arises: how can we experience *continual* victory? How can we come to the place where we steadfastly choose to act on the promptings of the Spirit rather than the promptings of the flesh? We have looked at some of the principles involved in learning to detect each impression quickly, evaluate it accurately, and then engage the will effectively. But we've also seen how Satan is waging an all out war against every piece of furniture in the sanctuary, a war designed to bring about our defeat and eventual destruction. Learning the right use of man's moral faculties can open up to us the possibility of a whole new experience of victory. But it takes more than information, we need power to use that information consistently.

WRITER'S BLOCK

When writing this book, I was enthusiastic about the prospect. I had been researching the information for many years, and had ample notes. I had presented the subject to many different groups and audiences and had a good idea how I wanted to present the material. In fact I had completed a rough draft of the first half of the book in just a week or two. I was even more excited about the second half of the book, and didn't expect it to take much longer. Then something struck: writer's block.

Actually, I don't know if that's the word for it. It just seems I hit an impasse and didn't now how to proceed. In fact, two whole weeks passed–without a single page being written. At first I thought it was normal busyness, just a strange convergence of bothersome interruptions that plague our lives every so often. But as it continued, I gradually began to realize there was a spiritual battle involved. So I prayed about it–and sensed there was an important component to understanding the sanctuary that needed to be included at this exact point in our study together. And that is the power of the Gospel.

TYPE AND ANTITYPE

You see, to understand the sanctuary, it is important to remember that it is a system of symbols. Enacted prophecies. Sometimes these are called types, and the fulfillment of those prophecies, antitypes. And while we cannot explore all the types in the Old Testament sanctuary system, one observation is critical. These sacrifices, ceremonies, rituals, and offerings, all pointed to the cross of Christ. This is what John the Baptist hinted at when he saw Jesus coming to him for baptism: "Behold the Lamb of God, which taketh away the sin of the world" (John 1:29). Jesus was the ultimate fulfillment of all those enacted prophecies carried out in the endless animal sacrifices of the ancient Hebrews. Christ was at the center of everything.

Or to put it a different way, we cannot really appreciate God's plan for victory in the life, without taking a few moments to see how Christ fits into the sanctuary. It may give us important insights into the nature of man, the physical, mental, and spiritual divisions of his being, the various faculties with which he has been endowed, and how they interrelate–but that picture is incomplete if the Gospel is not thoroughly interwoven through it all.

That is what was holding up the book. The sanctuary is not just a mechanistic schematic of our moral anatomy, it is a veiled Old Testament prophecy of the New Testament Gospel. In fact, without the fuller revelation of that Gospel, the sanctuary can give a misleading picture. Rather than a miracle of grace, victory becomes a formula. A formula that doesn't work. It is only as we take the meaning of the cross and superimpose it upon the sanctuary that we can grasp what God is really trying to teach us. In this chapter we will attempt to do just that. For a brief moment, we will work backwards–using the New Testament Gospel to shed light on the Old Testament principles we have studied so far.

WHAT IS THE GOSPEL?

Unfortunately, there are many different views on the Gospel. I won't attempt to critique the various theological schools of thought here–it would just add one more voice to the confusion. Rather, I'd like to keep things as simple as possible, and focus our study on how the Gospel works. The basics. The fundamentals. For however sophisticated our theology might be, if the Gospel doesn't make a difference in our life, it isn't worth much. When studying the topic of victory, it is not primarily information that we need, but the nuts and bolts of how to make that information function.

First and foremost, I'd like to suggest the Gospel involves power. Notice:

> *For the preaching of the cross is to them that perish foolishness; but unto us which are saved it is the power of God. I Corinthians 1:18*

In other words, the Gospel won't make much sense to someone who hasn't experienced it. In fact, the "theory" may seem a bit silly. But those who have personally encountered the cross of Christ, know first-hand that it has power to change a life.

Paul repeated this idea in several places, including this verse from the book of Romans:

> *For I am not ashamed of the gospel of Christ: for it is the power of God unto salvation to every one that believeth; to the Jew first, and also to the Greek. Romans 1:16*

Once again, the Gospel has saving, life-changing power. But note how that power is activated: through faith. It is power to those who believe. We will study the faculty of faith in a future chapter. For now, just observe that it is central to accessing power for victory.

In fact, if there was one theme running through all the miracles of Jesus, it would probably revolve around this issue of faith. When healing the two blind men in Matthew 9, He first asked, "believe ye that I am able to do this?" (vs. 28). And then He healed them saying, "according to your faith be it unto you" (vs. 29). When speaking to the father of the demon possessed boy in Mark 9, Jesus said something similar: "if thou canst believe, all things are possible to him that believeth" (Mark 9:23). To which the father wisely replied, "Lord, I believe; help thou mine unbelief" (vs. 24). In both these miracles and others like them, Jesus was trying to communicate the importance of faith in accessing divine power. So far so good.

THE SIN BEARER

The problem arises when we try to define exactly what we are to believe. In many Christian circles, it boils down to simply believing that Jesus died for our sins on the cross. That he paid the penalty we deserve for our long record of wrong choices. And this is certainly one aspect of faith.

The Bible clearly teaches we are under a penalty of death. "The wages of sin is death" (Romans 6:23). "The soul that sinneth, it shall die" (Ezekiel 18:4). And sadly, "all have sinned, and come short of the glory of God" (Romans 3:23). Apart from Christ, "there is none that doeth good, no, not one" (Psalms 14:3). This puts us all in a desperate situation.

And Christ is the sin bearer. As predicted in the Old Testament, "he was wounded for our transgressions, he was bruised for our iniquities; the chastisement of our peace was upon him . . . and the LORD hath laid on him the iniquity of us all" (Isaiah 53:5-6). In Christ, "we have redemption through his blood, even the forgiveness of sins" (Colossians 1:14). Christ "hath given himself for us an offering and a sacrifice to God" (Ephesians 5:2). "He is the propitiation for our sins" (I John 2:2). And in fact, "there is none other name under heaven given among men, whereby we must be saved" (Acts 4:12).[43]

---

43. Jesus said, "if ye believe not that I am he, ye shall die in your sins" (John 8:24). In this verse, the word "he" is supplied, suggesting we must see Christ as the great "I am." No other sacrifice would be sufficient to pay the price for man's sin.

One aspect of faith is to truly grasp that Christ *exhausted* the penalty we deserve. His sacrifice is complete and sufficient. There are no works of righteousness we could perform that would add one iota to the sacrifice of Christ. Nor is anything more needed. This point Paul argued repeatedly:

> *Therefore by the deeds of the law there shall no flesh be justified in his sight: Romans 3:20*

> *But that no man is justified by the law in the sight of God, it is evident: for, The just shall live by faith. Galatians 3:11*

Without faith in Christ as our sin bearer, we doom ourselves to a life of insecurity, fear, and lack of assurance. Religion becomes an endless round of dead works, striving to somehow earn more merit, yet never quite experiencing true peace with God.

A TWO-SIDED COIN

This faith in Christ as our sin bearer is only one aspect of the Gospel, however. The other side is exercising faith in Christ as a deliverer from the bondage of sin. I'm thankful the Gospel holds out the promise that my past sins can be erased, and remembered no more–but I'm even more thankful, perhaps, that it holds out the promise sin's ongoing power in my life can be broken.

Notice how John captured the essence of this two-sided Gospel in the following familiar verse:

> *If we confess our sins, he is faithful and just to forgive us our sins, and to cleanse us from all unrighteousness. I John 1:9*

There it is, the two parts: forgiveness AND cleansing. In other words, the Gospel provides a complete solution. It takes care of our past failures, and it provides power for our present, day to day challenges. In the New Covenant, God remembers our sins no more (past disobedience), but He also puts His Law into our heart and mind (present obedience).[44] I suspect it was especially this latter aspect–Christ's ability to dramatically transform our life through the Gospel–that Paul had in mind when he referred to it as "the power of God."

A UNITED GOSPEL

Theologians risk much when they try to break the Gospel down into different pieces. Like justification and sanctification. Or imputed and imparted righteousness. Forgiveness and transformation. As if they were two distinct things. In contrast, Scripture seems to blend them, more like two sides of a single coin. That is, there is one Gospel–and all its benefits are triggered by faith.

To put it differently, one cannot really exercise faith in Christ as the sin-bearer without also laying hold on Him as our sin-deliverer. The Gospel is not some single exchange (our sins for Christ's righteousness) that occurs at whatever point in our life we first trust Christ–it is a continuing connection. A continuing experience. Through the Gospel, Christ lives in me *today*.

---

44. *"This is the covenant that I will make with them after those days, saith the Lord, I will put my laws into their hearts, and in their minds will I write them; And their sins and iniquities will I remember no more." Hebrews 10:16-17.*

I probably first began to realize my "analytical" understanding of the Gospel was somewhat deficient years ago, when memorizing the following verse:

As ye have therefore received Christ Jesus the Lord, so walk ye in him: Colossians 2:6

Somehow I had just assumed the Gospel was something we did once, at "conversion", and that we then moved on to something else afterwards. It never occurred to me that the process by which we receive Christ is the exact same process by which we walk in Him, day by day. It took several more years before I understood what it looked like, to experience the Gospel as an ongoing power source, and not a one-time event.

Here's another way to think about it. Rather than viewing the Gospel primarily as something that adjusts God's record books, stamping pardon beside that long list of sins under our name, imagine the Gospel as something that moves us into a new relationship with Christ. We are "translated . . . into the kingdom of his dear Son" and thus "delivered . . . from the power of darkness" (Colossians 1:13). To receive the kingdom of forgiveness, is to live our life in a kingdom of deliverance. The two are inseparable.

Notice how important it is to keep this reality at the forefront of our consciousness:

Moreover, brethren, I declare unto you the gospel which I preached unto you, which also ye have received, and wherein ye stand; By which also ye are saved, if ye keep in memory what I preached unto you, unless ye have believed in vain. I Corinthians 15:1-2

To receive the Gospel, is to live our lives "standing" within it. And to enjoy the ongoing benefits of the Gospel, we must keep that reality fixed in our mind. We must cling to the fact we have not only been forgiven but transformed. After listing the various traits that should appear in the life of a believer, Peter adds, "he that lacketh these things is blind, and cannot see afar off, and hath forgotten that he was purged from his old sins" (II Peter 1:9). While claiming God's forgiveness, we must not lose sight of God's promised cleansing.

In another place, Paul explains that the same faith which moves us into a justified relationship with God, also unlocks our access to heaven's power:

> *Therefore being justified by faith, we have peace with God through our Lord Jesus Christ: By whom also we have access by faith into this grace wherein we stand, and rejoice in hope of the glory of God. Romans 5:1-2*

To receive forgiveness from Christ, and thus peace with God, is also to receive access to grace. That is, it opens the door to power. Power to stand. And keep standing. In fact, so much grace is available, it inspires the hope God's glory can be restored in man![45] In fact, Paul goes on to assure us this hope won't be "ashamed" thanks to the work of the "Holy Ghost" in our heart (vs 5). That's something to rejoice about for sure!

---

45. *Paul referred to what was possible through Christ in us as the "hope of Glory." Colossians 1:27. In another place, he said God has "called you by our gospel, to the obtaining of the glory of our Lord Jesus Christ." II Thessalonians 2:14. What a hope!*

THE GRACE OF GOD

The Gospel and grace are closely connected. In fact, Paul said his mission was to "testify the gospel of the grace of God" (Acts 20:24). The Gospel, it seems, is good news about grace. And not surprizingly, grace, like the Gospel, has two sides.

One side of grace, of course, is forgiveness: We are "justified freely by his grace through the redemption that is in Christ Jesus" (Romans 3:24). But it is also a transforming power. Paul wrote: "But by the grace of God I am what I am" (I Corinthians 15:10). He lived out his life in the world "by the grace of God" (II Corinthians 1:12). He was "made a minister, according to the gift of the grace of God" (Ephesians 3:7). And when challenged with infirmity, he gloried, knowing God's "grace is sufficient" (II Corinthians 12:9). In Paul's mind, grace was a living, active power. God is "able to make all grace abound toward you; that ye, always having all sufficiency in all things, may abound to every good work" (II Corinthians 9:8).

When we only see grace as pardon or unmerited favor, we miss the back side of the coin. Grace is also a supernatural energy or strength that is available to us moment by moment when we are in Christ. It is a "divine power" through which God gives "us all things that pertain unto life and godliness" (II Peter 1:3). A power any of us can tap into through the faculty of faith. It is the heartbeat of our walk with God. The Gospel is thus a continuous, moment by moment receiving of divine strength. Without faith in this kind of Gospel, transformation of the life is impossible.[46]

---

46. This is why Paul said, we "beseech you also that ye receive not the grace of God in vain." II Corinthians 6:1. Grace is available to all, but it must be mixed with faith to have any impact on the life. See Hebrews 4:2.

THE NITTY GRITTY

All this brings us down to the million dollar question. How does it actually work? I don't pretend to know the full answer to the question, nor do I profess to have attained perfect victory in every aspect of my life. But I will take a stab at an answer based on my experiences thus far.

First, it boils down to a state of mind. A sense of constant reliance on God. Of dependence on divine power. A steadfast looking to Jesus, combined with an expectation of assistance. Perhaps you could call it trust.

This state of mind is established on a foundation of three simple truths. The Gospel in a nutshell, so to speak. I often think of them as the ABC's of the Bible. Here they are:

> *Admit. Admit our inability to do right. It's called sin, and it is embedded right in our natures. We are in desperate need of help. And without assistance, we have no hope.*
>
> *Believe. Believe Christ exhausted the penalty we deserve. And as a result, we can have full forgiveness for sin. Christ's blood moves us into a new relationship with God, and grants us access to His grace.*
>
> *Claim. Claim the power of God for our life. Everything we need for right living is within our grasp. We only need to reach out and take hold of it. The power available is limitless.*

These truths are to become such a reality in our life that they are our automatic response to every situation. Our reaction to every circumstance. We are to live and breathe the Gospel.

THE PLACE OF PRAYER

It starts each morning by spending a few moments alone with God in prayer. The whole day lies before us. We know it will be filled with various trials and temptations. We will need grace to endure the one and resist the other. So we rush to our High Priest in prayer, for help:

> *Seeing then that we have a great high priest, that is passed into the heavens, Jesus the Son of God, let us hold fast our profession. For we have not an high priest which cannot be touched with the feeling of our infirmities; but was in all points tempted like as we are, yet without sin. Let us therefore come boldly unto the throne of grace, that we may obtain mercy, and find grace to help in time of need. Hebrews 4:14-16*

Think of this time as an opportunity to immerse your mind in the basic truths of the Gospel. Take at least a few moments each morning to review the ABC's—and then connect those truths to the major faculties of the sanctuary.

Your prayers might go something like this: "Lord, I need You today. You know I am weak. That I cannot resist sin on my own. I'm desperate for Your help. My eyes look to You." Then acknowledge any specific sins, weaknesses, or struggles the Holy Spirit brings to your mind. This is the admit stage. Next comes believe: "Thank You for Jesus, for the cross, for forgiveness. Thank You that the precious blood of Christ restores me to a right relationship with You, and grants me access to Your grace." Then one by one, yield each faculty to Christ—your conscience (and the other spiritual senses), your emotions, reason, the will, your actions, and even the desires of your flesh. Because of Christ's sacrifice alone, these offerings will be received by God. His blood makes each faculty "accepted in the beloved" (Ephesians 1:6). Finally, move on to claim, with something like the following: "Lord, grant me Your power today. Energize my spirit with Your Spirit. Sensitize my conscience to Your still small voice. Make my emotions more quick to discern Your every prompting. Ennoble my reason to correctly evaluate every impression by Your Word. Endow my will with divine energy that all its commands will be carried out in harmony with Your will. May all my actions be pleasing in Your sight. Help me to put my fleshly nature to death. Charge me up like a battery for today!" I'm not suggesting some memorized formula–what I'm suggesting is we need a daily experience in the Gospel.

THE MOMENT OF TRUTH

A daily prayer like this is just the beginning. It only prepares us for the battles of the day. Those battles still have to be fought! The key is knowing how to instantly turn to the Gospel at the moment of truth–when temptation hits. As noted already, we walk in Christ the same way we receive Him. The Gospel is supposed to be an ongoing moment by moment power source, for victory.

Imagine the chocolate cake once again. Senses on overload, the flesh crying out, your body preparing to reach out and take that piece you know you don't really need. If you prayed that morning you will be on the lookout for just such situations, and you will catch the whispered promptings of your conscience. At that moment you have two competing voices battling for control. It could go either way. What do you do?

Simple. Turn instantly to the Gospel. Flash a prayer to heaven along the lines of the ABC's. Admit: "Lord, You know I want this cake. I'm weak. There's a part of me that wants this. I need Your help." Believe: "Lord, thank You for Jesus, who died for me on the cross. I give myself to You once again, just now. I plead the blood of Christ–receive me." Claim: "Lord, by faith I claim Your power. I choose to turn away from this temptation. I trust You to grant me the strength I need." And then you act. You turn away from the piece of cake.

The entire prayer just takes a second or two. And it's not the words that count so much as the principles. We are looking to Christ. Turning to the cross. Laying hold of grace. The Gospel is not some past experience–it's living and breathing, right now, in the moment of truth. And it works.

Sometimes the victory will be easy. We simply turn from the temptation, and its influence is broken. At other times, we try to turn away, but then waiver. We find ourselves glancing back at the cake. What do we do then? Fire off another prayer to God. Round two: admit, believe and claim. "Lord You know I'm weak, I can't do this without Your help. I plead the blood of Christ. I come to You through the provisions of the cross. And just now I claim Your power to turn away. Help Lord, my unbelief!" And then try to turn a second time. Depending on the strength of the temptation it may take three or four rounds, or more. I've had times where I broke into a sweat from the heat of the battle.[47] But in all of my personal experiences with this

---

47. *The battle was so great in the Garden of Gethsemane, that Christ began to sweat "great drops of blood." Luke 22:44. And we are encouraged to meditate on this struggle when tempted: "For consider him that endured such contradiction of sinners against himself, lest ye be wearied and faint in your minds. Ye have not yet resisted unto blood, striving against sin." Hebrews 12:3-4.*

approach, I have discovered you cannot be overcome so long as you persevere in the battle. Ultimately, you will let go of the cake, or let go of the Gospel. It is as simple as that.[48]

THE GOSPEL WORKS

It really does. You can use the Gospel in virtually any situation. Not just sins of commission, like eating a piece of chocolate cake, but also sins of omission, like not wanting to get out of bed in the morning to study your Bible. You can use it when you are struggling with overwhelming negative emotions, fierce urges to rationalize, or as in our example, the battle for control of the will. It doesn't matter how big or small the temptation–the Gospel is all sufficient. It is truly the power of God to salvation!

Yes, there will be times you miss the "moment of truth" and carelessly yield without putting up a fight. There may even be times, for whatever reason, you simply choose to let go of the cross.[49] God never forces obedience. It must spring from a sincere desire on our part. But the experience of victory is sweet: Sensing a current of energy from heaven flow through our being. Learning experiential lessons of faith, reliance, and trust. Knowing first-hand the grace of God and the power of the Gospel–there is nothing like it. There will be ups and downs.

---

48. *I've heard it said, that the road to hell is blocked by the cross of Christ. A person must push that cross out of the way to be lost. There is a measure of truth in that saying.*

49. *Such a decision is extremely dangerous. Hebrews describes the experience of those who reject the cross of Christ, and how difficult it is "to renew them again unto repentance; seeing they crucify to themselves the Son of God afresh." Hebrews 6:4-6. For those who do this continually, repentance eventually becomes impossible.*

Starts and stops. But if you persevere, turning to Christ will gradually become more natural. Almost automatic. It becomes something of a state of mind. Our life becomes one of "prayer without ceasing" (I Thessalonians 5:17). And when this happens, at last, we will have the mind of Christ.

The sanctuary teaches us powerful lessons about man's moral machinery. But every compartment, and every piece of furniture must be bathed in the Gospel. When we do, we will see every victory, every success, every right choice stamped with the cross of Calvary. We will understand it is all only possible through Christ. And all glory and praise will go to Him!

Review Questions
Chapter 4–Power for Victory

1.   *Why is the Gospel important in understanding the sanctuary?*

2.   *What are the two sides of the Gospel? What are the risks in trying to separate them?*

3.   *In what ways is grace connected to the Gospel? How important is grace, and why?*

4.   *What are the three foundational truths of the Gospel?*

5.   *Explain what it means to immerse our self in the Gospel each morning. And at each moment of temptation.*

Understanding Character
Chapter 5

Ye are our epistle written in our hearts,
known and read of all men: Forasmuch as ye are
manifestly declared to be the epistle of Christ
ministered by us, written not with ink, but with
the Spirit of the living God; not in tables of stone,
but in fleshy tables of the heart.
II Corinthians 3:2-3

In the last two chapters we have focused primarily on the Holy Place of the sanctuary. That is, the faculties of the mind which are at the center of every inner battle between right and wrong: the emotions, reason, and the will. And how the key to continual victory is to continually immerse these faculties in the Gospel of grace. But I don't want to give the impression that the Christian life is all about conflict and warfare! True, there will be struggles and challenges as long as we live in this world. But the goal is actually transformation. To not only resist temptations, but to defeat them. To conquer challenges and then move on to new ones. This process is called growth. And to understand it properly, we must now turn to the Most Holy Place. We will need to explore what the Bible teaches about character.

Blessed is the man whose strength is in thee; in whose heart are [thy] ways . . . They go from strength to strength, every one of them. Psalms 84:5,7

But we all . . . are changed into the same image from glory to glory, even as by the Spirit of the Lord. II Corinthians 3:18

To put it a bit differently, we can gain real victory over specific temptations. Suppose your weakness is that proverbial chocolate cake. The temptations may be fierce, and frequent. But if each time we successfully turn to the cross, cling to grace, and resist the urge, those temptations will gradually grow weaker. In a process we will study shortly, that victory will becomes a part of our character. It somehow moves behind the veil and gets imprinted on the tables of the heart. And at that point, the temptation becomes minimal or even non-existent. There will be new temptations to face, of course, as our understanding of God's will for our life deepens, but the hold of that specific temptation on our life is broken. Christianity is not just about white-knuckling things, it is about real change: coming to the place where one temptation after another loses even its appeal. No doubt this is what Jesus meant when He said, "the prince of this world cometh, and hath nothing in me" (John 14:30).

IN THE BEGINNING

In the beginning, God created Adam with a character that was in harmony with heaven. As we've noted before, the "breath" that God blew into Adam's nostrils was in fact, spirit. His Spirit. His character. Every prompting of Adam's heart was in perfect unison with the Law of God. All the fruit of God's

Spirit were manifest in his life. Adam's character was initially formed in the image of God. And though largely effaced by 6000 years of sin, some of that image can still be seen. A trace of "the work of the law written in their heart" remains today (Romans 2:15).[50]

When Adam sinned, however, in eating the forbidden fruit, everything changed. "By one man sin entered into the world, and death by sin; and so death passed upon all men, for that all have sinned" (Romans 5:12). First, corruption came to man's body. Not just physical death, but a pull toward sin became mysteriously embedded in his body. And ever since, man has suffered under a curse of disease, pain, and death. "He that soweth to his flesh shall of the flesh reap corruption" (Galatians 6:8). Second, his mind became darkened. He allowed his emotions for Eve to overrule his reason in eating the fruit. He began to rationalize and justify a wrong course, and for the first time, his will was exercised to do something wrong.[51] And still today, man's tendency is to walk "in the vanity of their mind, having the understanding darkened, being alienated from . . . God" (Ephesians 4:17-18). But perhaps more significantly than either of these, Adam's spiritual nature was damaged. He was cast out of the garden, indicating a change in relationship with God. A new position. "Your iniquities have separated between you and your God" (Isaiah 59:2). His spiritual faculties were dulled. And for the first time in his life, a record of sin slipped behind the veil and was imprinted on the tables of his

---

50. In addition, his mind functioned properly, with nobility and integrity. And even the desires of his physical body were natural and wholesome. All three regions of the sanctuary were holy.

51. Paul makes it clear Adam was not deceived. See I Timothy 2:14. He understood the issues, and deliberately chose to disobey God.

heart. Adam's character was marred. No doubt many an angel shed tears at the once upright man now bent towards evil.

Fortunately the plan of salvation went into effect immediately. Jesus was "the Lamb slain from the foundation of the world" (Revelation 13:8). The provisions of the Gospel were made available to Adam at the precise instant of the fall, on the *promise* of Christ to become a sacrifice for sin. Though the cross was still far in the future, Adam had immediate access to grace through the blood of the atonement. Every resource was available for Adam to crucify the flesh, renew the mind, and pursue a godly character, just as those resources are available to us today. The Gospel is an "everlasting gospel" (Revelation 14:6).

NEWBORN BABES

Which brings us to the next point in our study: character and modern man. In many ways our experience is similar to fallen Adam.[52] Our flesh is corrupt, the mind is darkened, and our character scarred. The pull to sin in our physical body seems to be passed down directly from our parents as part of

---

52. *Christ too was born with a physical nature like ours. God sent "his own Son in the likeness of sinful flesh." Romans 8:3.*
"Forasmuch then as the children are partakers of flesh and blood, he also himself likewise took part of the same." Hebrews 2:14-18. But spiritually, Christ was "holy, harmless, undefiled, separate from sinners, and made higher than the heavens." Hebrews 7:26. In fact His Spirit was divine. As Romans puts it: "Jesus Christ . . . was made of the seed of David according to the flesh; And declared to be the Son of God with power, according to the spirit of holiness, by the resurrection from the dead." Romans 1:3-4. It was this combination of humanity with divinity that enabled Him to be " in all points tempted like as we are, yet without sin." Hebrews 4:15. Much of the confusion about Christ's nature disappears when we study it in the context of the sanctuary and the moral machinery.

our DNA. As noted in an earlier chapter, the "law of sin" is in the very "members" of our body (Romans 7:23-24). The mind comes to adopt certain thought patterns, emotional responses, habitual choices, based on the models we are exposed to as we grow. Our parents, siblings, and later our peers, friends, and associates. It is the old nature/nurture argument. One represents the problem in our body. The other, the problem in our mind. But what about the spirit or heart?

Many people believe the heart is corrupt from conception. However, the Bible makes it clear our spirits are not inherited from our parents, like our body. Notice the following verse:

> *Thou hidest thy face, they are troubled: thou takest away their breath, they die, and return to their dust. Thou sendest forth thy spirit, they are created: and thou renewest the face of the earth. Psalms 104:29-30.*

At death, our spirit goes back to God, and our body returns to the dust. At conception, God sends forth His Spirit, and a new, one-of-a-kind life is created. In other words, while your body comes from a mixture of the genetic features of your mother and father,[53] your spirit is a original, supernatural creation. God took a personal interest in your individual birth, and created you

---

53. *The Bible seems to indicate that God is also involved with the process by which our parents genes combine at our conception. "My substance was not hid from thee, when I was made in secret, and curiously wrought in the lowest parts of the earth. Thine eyes did see my substance, yet being unperfect; and in thy book all my members were written, which in continuance were fashioned, when as yet there was none of them." Psalms 139:15-16. I suspect God orchestrates a unique combination of physical strengths and weaknesses for each of us, specifically designed to help us develop a more Christlike character.*

to be a unique reflection of His glory. I do not personally believe that the spirit God implanted within you was initially defective in any way.

Think of the character as tables of soft clay. The tables of the heart.[54] At our conception, those tables are pretty much blank. But they are shaped in such a way as to be receptive to the moral Law. We've noted this several times. Or to use another familiar truism, every man is born with a God-shaped hole. There may also be certain elements of personality, or at least personality tendencies, implanted in man's spirit at conception. This is part of the uniqueness with which God endows every human being. The thing that makes us invaluable and irreplaceable. But more than anything else, it is an empty slate.

Unfortunately that slate gets marred very quickly. From infancy, the flesh begins clamoring. In fact the first thing a child learns to do well–is cry out when their little bodies want something. Because of the powerful sin nature in us, our minds are inclined to adopt the rationalizations, negative emotions, and selfish choices we are exposed to. And unless we are blessed with especially spiritual and discerning parents, our thought life quickly settles into patterns that are out of harmony with God. Wrong thoughts lead to wrong actions. And with each sin, a record of evil is imprinted on the heart.[55] As we age,

---

54. *We have used the KJV word, "table" several times in this book. A more accurate translation would be "tablet." Many ancient civilizations used soft clay tablets to record information using a stylus, in a writing system called cuneiform. When the clay was baked, it produced a permanent record. This is the imagery the Bible is trying to depict when it refers to the tables of the heart.*

55. *We will study the faculty of memory in our next chapter. It is an important spiritual faculty, and intimately involved in the formation of character. Every right and wrong choice records a memory in the heart. Our character is largely shaped by these memories.*

our sinful patterns become more firmly established and our sensitivity to divine impulses gradually diminish. The tables of the heart slowly harden into stone. Apart from the Gospel, this is the sad destiny of every man. A corrupt flesh, a darkened mind, and a scarred character.

GOSPEL OF FREEDOM

While we do not have space here to fully develop this thought, it is worth noting briefly, that the Gospel is often presented in the context of freedom. Jesus began His ministry, by announcing that His work was "to preach deliverance to the captives" (Luke 4:16). And later, He said those who continued in His Word would be "free indeed" (John 8:31-32,36). Similarly, Paul urged us to "Stand fast therefore in the liberty wherewith Christ hath made us free, and be not entangled again with the yoke of bondage" (Galatians 5:1). That bondage is perhaps best understood as the power of the flesh to bring our spirit into captivity. Note:

> For I delight in the law of God after the inward man: But I see another law in my members . . . bringing me into captivity to the law of sin which is in my members. O wretched man that I am! who shall deliver me from the body of this death? Romans 7:22-24.

Paul goes on to explain that we were "made subject to vanity, not willingly, but by reason of him [Satan] who hath subjected the same in hope" and that one day we "shall be delivered from the bondage of corruption into the glorious liberty of the children of God." Specifically, we wait for the "redemption of our body" (Romans 8:20-23).

Realizing that there is something precious, unique, and special within each of us, a spirit implanted within us by God Himself at conception, is an eye-opening revelation. It may be bound tightly in chains of sin, but there is a part of us longing to be free. To escape. It is irreplaceable in the eyes of God. Christ died on the cross to save that uniqueness which is you. And the cross gives us genuine hope.

GOOD & BAD HEARTS

If you ask many people what verse first comes to their mind when they think about the heart, it is often Jeremiah 17:9. "The heart is deceitful above all things, and desperately wicked: who can know it?" The assumption being, that this verse describes the condition of every person's heart. But such an assumption fails to take into account Christ's power to change our heart.[56]

The Bible, in fact, describes individuals as having many different kinds of hearts. It refers to blind hearts, hard hearts, foolish hearts, darkened hearts, proud hearts, perverse hearts, fearful hearts, faint hearts, wandering hearts, dull hearts, and more. But it also refers to individuals as having tender hearts, upright hearts, faithful hearts, willing hearts, and thankful hearts. Some prepared their hearts to seek God, others communed with God in their hearts, or received divine wisdom

---

56. *In this verse, Jeremiah was addressing a group of Jews with a specific problem. In the first verse of the chapter, we read "The sin of Judah is written with a pen of iron, and with the point of a diamond: it is graven upon the table of their heart." Jeremiah 17:1. This record of sin was what made their hearts so desperately wicked. Other verses describe individuals with hearts in harmony with the Law of God. Such hearts are described in positive terms.*

in their hearts to do some creative work. Some had purpose of heart, or had hearts that were firm as a stone (to do right). In fact, a good number of individuals are described as having a perfect heart. While we should never come to the point we conclude our character is perfect,[57] or even that we know our heart fully, we have to believe God has power to change hearts, if we are to exercise faith in that power!

Many of the parables Jesus told revolve around the fact people do indeed have different characters. Some are wheat, some are tares. There are both sheep and goats. Wise and foolish virgins. The four soils in the parable of the sower all represent different types of heart. If it is not possible for our heart to be changed, we are in a desperate situation. Only the "pure in heart" will see God (Matthew 5:8). Only those with an "honest and good heart" can respond properly to the Word (Luke 8:15). Only those with a "true heart" can draw near to Christ (Hebrews 10:22). Like David, our great longing should be: "Create in me a clean heart, O God; and renew a right spirit within me" (Psalms 51:10). But that prayer must be mixed with faith God can and will do it.[58] Ultimately, this is what God is looking for: "the eyes of the LORD run to and fro throughout the whole earth, to shew himself strong in the behalf of them whose heart is perfect toward him" (II Chronicles 16:9).

---

57. Paul strove to "win Christ" with this attitude: "Not as though I had already attained, either were already perfect: but I follow after." And then he adds for our benefit, "Let us therefore, as many as be perfect, be thus minded: and if in any thing ye be otherwise minded, God shall reveal even this unto you." Philippians 3:8-15.

58. Once again, we see the importance of faith. "The word preached did not profit them, not being mixed with faith in them that heard it." Hebrews 4:2.

EARLY TRAINING

What determines the kind of heart we have? Initially, it has much to do with our early training. Proverbs 22:6 says, "Train up a child in the way he should go: and when he is old, he will not depart from it." Or alternately, that training "will not depart from him." Either way, it is clear that childhood influences make a significant impact on the formation of character, and that character shapes how the life unfolds, "for out of it are the issues of life" (Proverbs 4:23).

In a classic work on Christian parenting, entitled "Child Guidance," we find a number of rich insights into this process of character formation. Like the Bible, the book hints at how our characters resemble soft "tables" that harden as we grow. "What the child sees and hears is drawing deep lines upon the tender mind, which no after circumstances of life can entirely efface." These impressions begin while the child is still in the womb. By the time they reach three years of age, "the foundation is laid" and by seven, their character is largely set.[59] In other words the experiences of early life make a lasting impression, much like someone carving their initials into wet cement with a stick. Once dried into concrete, those letters are there for good.

The book also describes the process by which character is formed. Notice the steps involved:

---

59. "During the first three years of their lives . . . the foundation is laid." "The lessons that the child learns during the first seven years of life have more to do with forming his character than all that it learns in future years." Child Guidance, p. 194, 193.

Any one act, either good or evil, does not form the character, but thoughts and feelings indulged prepare the way for acts and deeds of the same kind. It is by a repetition of acts that habits are established and character confirmed.[60]

The "thoughts and feelings indulged" point to the mind: reason, the emotions, and the will. In another place, it is described as "the thoughts and feelings cherished." The same three faculties. The "acts and deeds" that result point to the body. But it is not isolated thoughts or acts that shape the character. It is habitual thoughts and habitual actions. Again, from a different section of the book:

Character does not come by chance . . . It is not determined by one outburst of temper, one step in the wrong direction. It is the repetition of the act that causes it to become habit, and molds the character either for good or for evil.[61]

Once again, we see that it is repetition that molds the character. And this character, established in our early years, shapes the life.

If parents are spiritual and discerning, they will help the child to think right thoughts, have cheerful emotions, and make noble choices, until these patterns become habitual and sink down into their character. More important, they will teach their children to turn to Christ, and lean on the power of the Gospel moment by moment. In so doing, they impart a character that tends toward continual victory. In most cases however, parents

---

60. *Child Guidance, p. 199.*

61. *Child Guidance, p. 164.*

will model their own defects of character: their tendency to gratify the flesh, compromise the will, rationalize, and indulge in negative emotions. This is what the child sees and hears. And imitates. Over time these patterns are reproduced from generation to generation. By beholding, the child is changed.[62]

This helps to explain a rather puzzling verse right in the heart of the second commandment: "I the LORD thy God am a jealous God, visiting the iniquity of the fathers upon the children unto the third and fourth generation" (Exodus 20:5). It is not that God punishes children for their parent's sins,[63] rather sinful patterns are passed down from parent to child. The children then repeat the mistakes of their parents, and suffer the same or similar consequences. The details and circumstances will vary, but the underlying character tendencies are reproduced. They are transferred from one table to another, from one generation to the next.

GOD'S PLAN FOR PARENTING

If you were not raised in a Christian home, or your parents failed to model a biblical character for you in your childhood, this may seem like a serious disadvantage. And it is. However, pause for a moment to think about the other side of

---

62. By "beholding as in a glass the glory of the Lord" we "are changed into the same image from glory to glory, even as by the Spirit of the Lord." II Corinthians 3:18. Where we focus our spiritual eyes, will determine the character we develop.

63. Ezekiel 18:20 says, "The soul that sinneth, it shall die. The son shall not bear the iniquity of the father, neither shall the father bear the iniquity of the son: the righteousness of the righteous shall be upon him, and the wickedness of the wicked shall be upon him." Clearly, no one is counted guilty because of the actions of another. We are each accountable for our own individual choices.

the issue. What if you had been raised in such a home? In other words, this process by which character is formed can just as surely lead to good results as it can to poor ones.

Suppose Adam and Eve had never sinned. Their offspring would have been exposed to nothing but righteousness, and each child would have formed a character just as in tune with heaven as their parents. And generation after generation, that godly character could have been passed down securely. Even in our world today, godly parents who have experienced character transformation themselves have the privilege of partnering with Christ in passing those same traits of character on to their children. Each child, in time, will have to make a personal decision for Christ, but their parents can impart principles of honesty, diligence, patience and purity that will make such a choice easier and more natural. And even if they do choose to reject the Savior, this early training will still prove a strength to them, through their entire lives.

God's intention was for parents to understand and take advantage of this process of character development in raising their children. Notice His instructions to parents:

> *Hear, O Israel: The LORD our God is one LORD: And thou shalt love the LORD thy God with all thine heart, and with all thy soul, and with all thy might. And these words, which I command thee this day, shall be in thine heart. Deuteronomy 6:4-6*

The first priority of parents is to make God first in each facet of their own life: the spiritual, mental and physical. And to do this the Word of God must be internalized in their own heart and life. In other words, before they can parent effectively, they must have a living experience in the Gospel themselves. They must cultivate a Christlike character if they are to model it before their children. Now the next few verses:

> *And thou shalt teach them diligently unto thy children, and shalt talk of them when thou sittest in thine house, and when thou walkest by the way, and when thou liest down, and when thou risest up. And thou shalt bind them for a sign upon thine hand, and they shall be as frontlets between thine eyes. And thou shalt write them upon the posts of thy house, and on thy gates. Deuteronomy 6:7-9*

It is easy to gloss over the meaning of these verses. But imagine growing up in such a home. The first thing your parents do when you get up in the morning is talk about the Law of God. You talk about it every time you sit down to a meal. Every time you go out for a walk. Your parents have a copy of the Law strapped on their hand, and on their forehead. You see a copy when you walk out the front door of your house, and then again at the gate, down by the road. It is the last thing your parents talk to you about when you go to bed at night. Everywhere, it is the Law of God.

Why did God command such a radical method of child training? As noted above, "what the child sees and hears is drawing deep lines upon the tender mind, which no after circumstances of life can entirely efface." In other words, by constant exposure and diligently repeated instruction, the Law is being imprinted into the child's character. They are being trained to live a godly life, with cheerful emotions, principled reasoning, and uncompromising integrity. It is our privilege as parents to raise such children.

CONVERSION & CHARACTER

But what about me? What if I wasn't raised in such a home, and blessed with such childhood training? What hope do I have, if my early influences were less than ideal, and the defects of my character are now set in stone? Apart from a miracle of God, the situation sounds pretty desperate!

It is. We were designed in such a way, that the patterns we pick up during those first years of life shape our character, permanently. Without some divine intervention, we have little option but to endlessly struggle against the exact same issues year after year. But there is divine intervention! The second commandment not only describes the law of generations, it also holds out hope:

> *I the LORD thy God am a jealous God, visiting the iniquity of the fathers upon the children unto the third and fourth generation of them that hate me; And shewing mercy unto thousands of them that love me, and keep my commandments. Exodus 20:5-6*

So there is a way out! There is a means by which we can escape the destiny of our faulty training and receive mercy. That means, of course, is the Gospel.

You see, the Gospel not only provides forgiveness for the past sins of the body. Not only does it provide grace for the renewing of the mind. But it provides a means by which the character can be restored. It works a supernatural miracle at the spiritual level. It is a complete solution!

In fact, conversion is primarily a spiritual transformation. There will be new mental patterns of course, and with improved lifestyle choices, there will likely be improved physical fitness and better health. But these are by-products of a heart change. God's Spirit comes into our spirit and begins to awaken new impulses. We see things through new eyes as our spiritual senses begin to awaken. And most importantly, something happens to the heart itself:

> *A new heart also will I give you, and a new spirit will I put within you: and I will take away the stony heart out of your flesh, and I will give you an heart of flesh. And I will put my spirit within you. Ezekiel 36:26-27*

Notice that the entrance of the Holy Spirit does not initially change what is written on the tables–rather, it changes the substance from which our tables are made. It turns them from stone to flesh. Our hearts become tender and soft once more, much like a little child.[64] And thus, there is now the *potential* for character change. It is as if hard concrete could somehow become wet cement again, making it possible to smooth out the defects. This is the glorious hope of the Gospel.

Paul described what becomes possible as a result of this transformation of the heart in these words:

> *Ye are manifestly declared to be the epistle of Christ ministered by us, written not with ink, but with the Spirit of the living God; not in tables of stone, but in fleshy tables of the heart. II Corinthians 3:3*

Paul only considered himself an agent in this process; it was the Holy Spirit that did the rewriting of the heart. But note the Holy

---

64. *Perhaps this is what Jesus meant when he said "Verily I say unto you, Whosoever shall not receive the kingdom of God as a little child, he shall not enter therein." Mark 10:15. The character must become soft and moldable as a child, in order to be rewritten.*

Spirit could only write new content on tables that had first been changed from stone to flesh. Without that transformation, the Holy Spirit can no more write on our hearts, than we can write on hardened concrete.

But note that this rewriting of the heart is a process. It does not all happen instantly, without any effort or cooperation on our part. We do not go to bed one night with a badly damaged character and wake up the next morning with instant, simultaneous victory over every defect! The transformation of heart, from stone to flesh, happens instantly–the moment we put true faith in Christ. And power for victory over every temptation is also immediately available through the provisions of the Gospel. We studied that power in our last chapter. But full freedom from temptation, the rewriting of lifelong patterns and habits takes time.

And we have a part in that process. That part involves a retraining of the character, using the same principles by which character is trained in the first place. Notice the similarities between the following verses and God's plan for parenting as noted earlier:

> *My son, keep my words, and lay up my commandments*
> *with thee. Keep my commandments, and live; and my law*
> *as the apple of thine eye. Bind them upon thy fingers,*
> *write them upon the table of thine heart. Proverbs 7:1-3*

While it is the Holy Spirit that does the actual rewriting, we can cooperate with God by focusing our mind on spiritual things. Just like parents who continually expose their children to the Law of God, we are to lay up Scripture in our minds, and meditate on it constantly. That is, by faithfully memorizing the Word of God, (memory is one of our spiritual faculties), we give the Holy Spirit something to work with. He can then take those principles, stamp them into the character, and ultimately change the life.

The phrase "apple of thine eye" used in the passage above can perhaps be better translated as "the little man of the eye." Have you ever looked so closely into another person's eyes, that you saw your own image reflected there? The Hebrew expression used is an idiom describing that experience. It captures the idea of what we must do with God's commandments. We must keep them so close before our eyes, that we see our self reflected in them continuously. Our emotions, reason, the will, our actions: everything must be viewed through the lens of God's Word. And this is why memorization is so vital–both in training our children, and in retraining ourselves. It allows us to have passages of Scripture with us at all times, and intertwine them into the daily activities of our life.

Remember, character is not determined by isolated thoughts or actions, but by habitual, repeated thoughts and actions. By internalizing Scripture, the spiritual impulses are strengthened, but there must be victory for a sustained period of time, where the emotions, reason and will respond to those promptings through the grace of God, leading to action. New habits and patterns must be established. The Gospel sustains our victory during this time. But eventually, the Holy Spirit will take those principles and implant them in the character. Victory will become easier and easier. Like Jesus, we will be able to say, "I delight to do thy will, O my God: yea, thy law is within my heart" (Psalms 40:8). We have changed.

AN ILLUSTRATION

Imagine a young woman. She is polite, pleasant, and attractive. But deep down, she feels inadequate, ugly, worthless. All through her childhood, her parents said hurtful things to her. Demeaning her. Shaming her. They failed to affirm and nurture her. Given such a situation, it should not be surprising she struggles with negative emotions, and poor self-esteem. Even if friends give her a compliment, she will not believe them, because her heart is shouting something different. The character formed in those early years controls her life still, as an adult.

Remember how the emotions are like a window to the inner man? In this sense, even negative emotions have value, because they highlight the fact there are problems behind the veil. They are like a blinking red light on the dashboard of your car. We may not know exactly where the problem is, but it is dangerous to ignore the signal. Something back there needs to be repaired, and quick! And disconnecting the warning light, won't solve things either. There will be problems in our life, and continued negative emotions until the root cause, the character, is fixed.

Suppose now that our struggling friend at some point becomes a Christian. She invites Christ into her heart and surrenders her life to His leading. Is her character instantly changed? Are all her inner struggles immediately resolved? No. But her heart becomes tender, and she begins to sense the Lord's promptings more clearly. Gradually she comes to understand the power of the Gospel and begins to experience victories in specific areas of her life. But the negative thoughts and feelings are harder to shake. They are rooted more deeply, and they continue to plague her.

In time, the Holy Spirit will begin to impress her that these issues need to be addressed. Lovingly He directs her mind to specific passages of Scripture, that affirm her value and worth in the sight of God. And He prompts her to memorize them. There is no sudden change in her life. She continues to have her ups and downs, but she continues to pray, study, memorize, and meditate under the leading of the Holy Spirit. Eventually, there is a critical mass of God's Word in her heart.

Perhaps one day she has had some particularly trying encounter, and she finds herself out walking in a park, tears streaming down her cheeks. All her feelings of hurt and rejection raging in her mind. Suddenly she hears the Spirit of God whispering to her:

> *Yea, I have loved thee with an everlasting love: therefore with lovingkindness have I drawn thee. Jeremiah 31:3*

It takes her by surprise. Yes, she knows the verse, but could it actually be true? Before she can take another breath, another verse flashes into her mind:

> *Thou wast precious in my sight, thou hast been honourable, and I have loved thee. Isaiah 43:4*

Is God truly speaking to me? Has He really noticed my hurting heart? And then without giving her a moment to react, another verse comes crashing in:

> *How precious also are thy thoughts unto me, O God! how great is the sum of them! If I should count them, they are more in number than the sand. Psalms 139:17-18*

And then another, and another. Suddenly the tears change from tears of pain to tears of joy. It's true. It really is. I'm loved of God. I'm precious. I have value. The words she has memorized have begun to sink down into her character. She begins to believe them with her heart. She is changing.

It will take some time, of course, for every trace of her old patterns to be replace with new ones. She will have to persevere in keeping her mind fixed on the truths of the Bible, as the little man of her eye. And she will have to wage fierce Gospel battles while she waits for those broken tables of her heart to be fully rewritten. But if she perseveres, her personal experience will shift more and more from fights to freedom. If she continues in the Word, she will one day be free indeed.

Whether we are struggling with negative emotions, false beliefs, or a powerless will, the process is the same. Come to Christ. Learn how to tap into the power of Gospel, and begin resisting the old sin patterns. But simultaneously, begin cooperating with God in the retraining of your character. Prayerfully study what the Bible has to say about your specific area of struggle and memorize every verse you can. Then keep those verses running through your mind throughout the day. Give God time to work. An exciting new character will be yours at last!

This is the covenant that I will make with them after those days, saith the Lord, I will put my laws into their hearts, and in their minds will I write them; And their sins and iniquities will I remember no more. Hebrews 10:16-17

Review Questions
Chapter 5–Understanding Character

1. *Describe Adam's condition at creation. What changes took place at the fall?*

2. *Explain what the Bible teaches about the spirit of man. Where does it come from? What happens to it at death?*

3. *Give examples of different kinds of hearts mentioned in the Bible. Why is it important to believe hearts can change?*

4. *Explain the process by which character is formed? How can parents cooperate with God in training their children?*

5. *How does conversion affect our heart? What is our part in developing a more Christlike character?*

Life in the Spirit
Chapter 6

Thou wilt shew me the path of life:
in thy presence is fulness of joy;
at thy right hand there are pleasures for evermore.
Psalms 16:11

The wise man, Solomon, gave an important warning in Ecclesiastes 12:12, "of making many books there is no end; and much study is a weariness of the flesh." This warning is particularly true when studying the spiritual senses. There is so much one could say about these four senses, a person could write an entire book about each of them. I've toyed with the idea myself! In the meantime, however, we must content ourselves with a mere survey. In previous chapters I have tried to be a bit more comprehensive; but here we are just scratching the surface.

THE SPIRITUAL SENSES

So far we have seen how the sanctuary is a map or blueprint of man's moral machinery, and explored some of the connections between it, and how God has made us. We have looked at the three main divisions of man: body, mind, and heart, and seen how they correspond to the three regions of the sanctuary. We have also examined the battle that takes place between the spirit and the flesh, and how that battle is fought through the primary faculties of the mind: reason, the emotions, and the will. Victory is dependent on immersing these faculties in the Gospel. And more recently, we have explored what the Bible teaches about character. How it is originally shaped, and how it can be re-shaped. All of these topics are vital in living the Christian life.

In this chapter we will look at the faculties of the Most Holy Place in more detail. What we have referred to as our spiritual senses. Much like our physical senses, which pick up information about the physical world, and convey that knowledge to the mind, our spiritual senses detect information about the spiritual realm, and convey that knowledge to the mind. It often comes in the form of promptings or impressions. Understanding how these senses work, and learning to tap into the messages they are sending is the secret to living a Spirit-filled life. For ultimately, it is in acting on these messages that all true obedience, spiritual growth and character development takes place.

Learning to tap into our spiritual senses, is like opening our eyes or unplugging our ears. Our life becomes filled with excitement, wonder, and adventure. Here is how Paul described this reality:

> *The inward man is renewed day by day. For our light affliction, which is but for a moment, worketh for us a far more exceeding and eternal weight of glory; While we look not at the things which are seen, but at the things which are not seen: for the things which are seen are temporal; but the things which are not seen are eternal.*
> *II Corinthians 4:16-18*

No matter how difficult or trying our external day to day life might be, the inner man is renewed when we view life through the spiritual senses. It gives strength and courage to the mind, and fills the life with glory. Our spiritual senses are the key to all this and more.

FOUR PILLARS

As noted in earlier chapters, both our physical and spiritual senses can be represented by the pillars in the temple. To pass between the Outer Court to the Holy Place, one had to go through the door, a thick curtain suspended by five pillars. In a similar way, the body transmits data to the mind through five primary senses: sight, sound, taste, touch and smell.

The Holy Place and Most Holy Place were separated by a second curtain called the veil. It was suspended by four pillars, suggesting four spiritual senses. In my study of the moral machinery, I have found four specific faculties directly linked to the heart or spirit of man. And each of them can be linked directly to the Ark of the Covenant, the one piece of furniture in the Most Holy Place. Which suggests they are four facets of a single process–and indeed, all four work in almost identical ways. In other words, it is as if the Bible has given us four different labels, all describing the same thing: The working of the Holy Spirit in the human heart.[65] It is one piece of furniture, yet four pillars.

---

65. *The Bible also uses many metaphors based on our physical senses: "Taste and see that the Lord is good" "A savor [smell] of life unto life, and of death unto death" "If they might haply feel after God and find Him" "If any man have an ear to hear, let him hear" "Seeing that which is invisible". More examples could be given.*

In the pages ahead we will look briefly at each of these spiritual faculties. They include the conscience, memory, love and faith.

THE CONSCIENCE

We have discussed the conscience already in a number of places. Like the other spiritual faculties, the conscience is similar to a physical sense organ, admitting information into the mind–only it picks up spiritual messages. These messages come in two forms: it accuses, when we do something contrary to the Law of God, and it excuses when our course is right, especially in the face of opposition. These are registered as the emotions of guilt or sorrow for sin, and joy or peace with God. The Bible directly connects the conscience with the workings of the heart, and the inclination in the heart of man, however weak, toward the Law of God. The Ten Commandments of course, were kept inside the Ark of the Covenant, in the Most Holy Place. And in the innermost region of every man, there are "tables of the heart" shaped in such a way to receive the Law of God. Though sin ends up getting imprinted on these tables instead, to one extent or another, there is still a part of us that is attracted to righteousness. We call that attraction the conscience.

On a side note, I should mention here that spiritual truth comes to man through the conscience. That is, this sense organ has a special ability to discern the voice of God. Which has profound implications for ministry. Many speakers today appeal to various mental faculties: the emotions via dramatic, moving stories, or the reason with impressive logic and evidence, or the will through long drawn out altar calls. Each has its place–but spiritual truth is perceived primarily through the spirit, not the mind. Paul writes, "But the natural man receiveth not the things of the Spirit of God: for they are foolishness unto him: neither can he know them, because they are spiritually discerned. But he that is spiritual judgeth all things" (I Corinthians 2:14-15). Paul's goal in preaching was to avoid all manipulation ("dishonesty," "craftiness," and "deceit"), and focus instead on the "manifestation of the truth commending ourselves to every man's conscience in the sight of God" (II Corinthians 4:1-2).[66] Paul relied first and foremost on the conviction of the Holy Spirit to bring his points home to his hearers. And the more consistently we learn to hush the other competing voices clamoring for attention in our mind, the more we will be able to discern truth today.

Part of the transformation that takes place at conversion involves the conscience. Twice in the book of Hebrews, the writer describes the Old Testament sacrifices as being inadequate, because they left us with a "conscience of sins" (Hebrews 9:9, 10:2). The blood of Christ, in contrast, is able to "purge your conscience from dead works to serve the living God" (Hebrews 9:14). Through Christ, we can draw near to God, "having our hearts sprinkled from an evil conscience" (Hebrews 10:22). There is something about the wondrous sacrifice of Christ, beholding Him on the cross, that awakens our moral sensitivities. It makes the heart, hardened by a lifetime of habitual and repeated sins, become tender and responsive once again. It changes from stone to flesh.

---

66. Elsewhere Paul suggests that to hold "the mystery of the faith" one must have "a pure conscience" and that the ones who give "heed to seducing spirits and doctrines of devils" are those who have had "their conscience seared." I Timothy 3:9, 4:1-2. Jesus said our ability to know truth depends on our willingness to obey it. "If any man will do his will, he shall know of the doctrine." John 7:17

To keep the conscience tender, it is important to resist temptation. Every time we violate the conscience we risk becoming desensitized to sin. That is, it grows stronger or weaker with every victory, every defeat. We have already discussed the process of temptation, and the secret to victory, in previous chapters–so we won't say much more about that here. But there is another aspect to strengthening the conscience worth looking at. Not only does the Bible describe the conscience as being defiled or pure, depending on whether or not it is "void of offence" (Acts 24:16), but it is also described as weak or strong based on how much knowledge a person has. In other words, the conscience can be educated.[67]

Or to put it differently, the conscience is not always completely reliable. It is never safe to disregard the voice of conscience. It is one of the chief means God uses to speak to us. Rather, we should be constantly striving to increase our sensitivity to right and wrong. But we must remember that all spiritual promptings need to be tested and evaluated by Scripture. Sometimes we are raised in such a way that we come to believe something is good or bad, when in fact, God sees it exactly the opposite. Or we form convictions from personal beliefs based on faulty information and as a result get misguided messages back from the conscience. We are all shaped by upbringing, culture, education and various life

---

67. Curiously enough, every instance of a "weak conscience" in the Bible, is connected with individuals who were convicted about things that were not actually wrong. That is, a weak conscience biblically, is one that is over-sensitive, due to a lack of knowledge. Spiritual maturity frees us from a religion of "touch not; taste not; handle not;" "which things have indeed a shew of wisdom in will worship" but are in fact works "of the flesh." See Colossians 2:20-23. Wisdom and understanding bring true freedom in Christ.

experiences. These shape our character and as a result mold the conscience. God's voice is always true, but our hearing can distort the message. The goal is thus to improve our hearing!

That means educating the conscience. To do this, I would encourage an ongoing and thorough study of the Law of God. The Ten Commandments are a beautiful and profound look into the heart of Christ, who was the embodiment of the principles of the Law. Isaiah, prophesying of Christ, wrote "he will magnify the law, and make it honourable" (Isaiah 42:21). The Bible makes it clear, the commandments do not just extend to the actions, but to the "secret" thoughts and intents of the heart (Ecclesiastes 12:13-14). Until we learn to study the commandments in this way, they will remain a collection of do's and don'ts. But they can become a powerful portrait of a Christlike life.

This is how Jesus taught us to study the Law. In the Sermon on the Mount, for example, He said it wasn't enough to avoid killing people–to be angry with someone was to put us "in danger of the judgment" (Matthew 5:21-22). He also gave specific instruction on how to resolve differences and seek reconciliation. As long as we live in this world, we will be wronged by others, and experience pain. How we respond says something about our character. If it is with forgiveness, our character is like Christ. If with bitterness, it is not. In other words, embedded right in the heart of the sixth commandment is the biblical principle of forgiveness.

Jesus also mentioned the next commandment, explaining that a person can commit adultery "in his heart" by simply "looking on a woman" in an impure way (Matthew 5:27-28). In other words, the commandment is not just about the act of adultery, it is a call to purity of thought and character. In fact,

Jesus goes on to explain that anything which contributes to the dissolution of the marriage bond is ultimately a violation of the commandment (vs 31-32). This can include whether we treat our spouse in such a way as to bind their heart to ours, or we push them away. Even our dating practices before marriage can enhance or damage our chance of a successful future union. All this is implied when we look to the spirit of the Law.

Understanding the spirituality of the Law goes far beyond these two examples. The command to honor our parents, involves our attitudes toward authority in every context of life (work, government, church, marriage, etc). To not bear false witness, is more than telling an outright lie. Sometimes it is an exaggeration, or even an omission. Sometimes the masks we wear are a lie. Sometimes we lie to our self! The command to make God first in our life extends to any thing that competes for first place in our life. And God's greatest competitor is self. We can go through each of the commandments in this way–searching for underlying principles that extend to the very core of our being. As the Bible says: "thy commandment is exceeding broad" (Psalms 119:96). And again, "Wherefore the law is holy, and the commandment holy, and just, and good" (Romans 7:12).

As noted at the beginning of this chapter, a book could easily be written on this topic. We don't have space here. I only wish to encourage you to begin a life-long study of the moral principles contained in the decalogue. It is a fascinating study, and the more your understanding grows of the revealed will of God, the more sensitive, and better educated, your conscience will be.

MEMORY

I was giving a talk one time at a wonderful Christian school in the western part of Canada, when the principal, a personal friend of mine came up and asked me a question. I had been talking about the sanctuary and its parallels to our design as humans, and had already identified the various compartments and pieces of furniture. His question was, "What about the pot of manna, and Aaron's rod? What do they represent?" I had never thought about it, up to that point, and could only give him a blank look. Eventually, I came to realize these two objects were stored in the Ark of the Covenant,[68] side by side with the Ten Commandments, as *memorials* of important events in the experience of Israel when it came out of Egypt. In other words, they represent memory. Also stored in "the side of the Ark," was a copy of the Torah, the first five books of Moses.[69] These books included a complete record of the history of the children of Israel from their deliverance out of Egypt, to their entrance into the promised land. This too, certainly implies memory.

We have already seen how memory is connected with the Most Holy Place. The experiences of life, especially those events of early childhood, get imprinted in the heart, behind the veil–and these memories play an important part in the formation of character. In fact, the expression "tables of the heart" is commonly used in the Bible to refer to memory. Clearly it is a faculty of the innermost part of the sanctuary. And it makes sense, when you recall that the veil between the Holy Place and Most Holy Place was the partition between our

---

68. *See Hebrews 9:4. See also Exodus 16:33 and Numbers 17:10.*

69. *See Deuteronomy 31:24-26.*

conscious mind and unconscious spirit. Imagine what it would be like to be conscious of every memory stored in your head, simultaneously. It's one thing to be able to retrieve a specific memory at a specific time, as needed. But to have thousands of memories all blaring in our mind at the same time–it would be insanity. No, memories are stored away back in our unconscious, back behind the veil.

Which explains how memory is like a sense organ. Suppose we are about to do or say something unwise, and suddenly a memory flashes into our mind of some similar situation, where our choice resulted in a negative consequence. We pause for a moment, evaluate the similarities between the two situations, and then decide to make a different, hopefully better choice. Just like promptings of the conscience, memories frequently pop into our mind to encourage some action, give a warning or caution, or simply to deepen our understanding of whatever we are thinking about.

We are specifically told that this is one of the ways the Holy Spirit works. "The Holy Ghost, whom the Father will send in my name, he shall teach you all things, and bring all things to your remembrance, whatsoever I have said unto you" (John 14:26). In other words, the Holy Spirit speak to us through the things we have stored in our memory, bringing just what is needed to our mind, at just the right time.[70] These impressions need to be tested and verified, just like any other

---

70. *"Jesus promised His disciples: 'The Comforter, which is the Holy Ghost, whom the Father will send in My name, He shall teach you all things, and bring all things to your remembrance, whatsoever I have said unto you.' John 14:26. But the teachings of Christ must previously have been stored in the mind in order for the Spirit of God to bring them to our remembrance in the time of peril." Great Controversy, p. 600.*

impression,[71] but it is definitely one means through which God communicates to us. "And thine ears shall hear a word behind thee, saying, This is the way, walk ye in it, when ye turn to the right hand, and when ye turn to the left" (Isaiah 30:21).

Of course we have a part in strengthening this faculty as well. The best approach is to begin a program of systematic Bible memorization. Repeatedly in Scripture we are commanded to store Scripture in our minds.[72] "Therefore shall ye lay up these my words in your heart and in your soul." "Receive, I pray thee, the law from his mouth, and lay up his words in thine heart." "My son, keep my words, and lay up my commandments with thee . . . write them upon the table of thine heart" (Deuteronomy 11:18, Job 22:22, Proverbs 7:1,3). Memorizing Scripture fills the tables of our heart with God's Word, making it available for the Holy Spirit's use at a moment's notice. The Holy Spirit will be faithful to bring it to remembrance just when it is needed, but we must be faithful to first get it stored in the memory![73]

---

71. *No two circumstances are identical in every particular. We need divine wisdom if we are to apply lessons learned in past experiences to new situations properly. Memory can suggests a course, but reason must determine if that course is in harmony with God's will.*

72. *Also important is remembering significant interventions by God in our life. The Hebrews were not only commanded to review their deliverance from Egypt, but to pass the stories on to their children. "Only take heed to thyself, and keep thy soul diligently, lest thou forget the things which thine eyes have seen, and lest they depart from thy heart all the days of thy life: but teach them thy sons, and thy sons' sons." Deuteronomy 4:9.*

73. *For more information about how to memorize Scripture effectively, please visit our website at WWW.FAST.ST and take our free Crash Course in Bible Memorization.*

But the initial memorization is only the first step. It must be combined with constant review and meditation. The things that pop into our mind most often, are generally the things we have been thinking about recently. Review keeps the verses we memorize fresh and accessible. Meditation helps us to connect those verses to specific situations and events, which helps bring those verses to mind whenever we find ourselves in a similar setting. Rote memorization of a verse is helpful, but it becomes far more valuable when we take the time to digest a verse and connect its principles to real life.

The Bible promises wonderful blessings to those who memorize and meditate on Scripture: "This book of the law shall not depart out of thy mouth; but thou shalt meditate therein day and night, that thou mayest observe to do according to all that is written therein: for then thou shalt make thy way prosperous, and then thou shalt have good success" (Joshua 1:8). "Blessed is the man [whose] delight is in the law of the LORD; and in his law doth he meditate day and night. And he shall be like a tree planted by the rivers of water, that bringeth forth his fruit in his season; his leaf also shall not wither; and whatsoever he doeth shall prosper" (Psalms 1:1-3). Amazing promise! Whatever you do will prosper? It is true, because constant memorization and meditation will shape the character, and "out of it are the issues of life" (Proverbs 4:23).

Before continuing on, it is important to make one additional observation about memory. And that is, our memories need to be filtered. Like conscience, the memories that flash into our mind are not infallible. In fact, it is common for people to struggle with negative memories, constantly rehearsing in their mind painful experiences from the past. Paul urges us to focus our thoughts on things that are true, honest, just, pure, lovely, of good report, virtuous, and worthy of praise

(Philippians 4:8). Sometimes memories need to be resisted: "this one thing I do, forgetting those things which are behind, and reaching forth unto those things which are before, I press toward the mark for the prize of the high calling of God in Christ Jesus" (Philippians 3:13-14). God says, "remember ye not the former things, neither consider the things of old. Behold, I will do a new thing" (Isaiah 43:18-19). It is difficult to eject painful memories by trying not to think about them. The solution is to replace them with new thoughts. And memorizing Scripture is a powerful weapon in this area as well. To maximize the faculty of memory, we must learn to focus on God's promises of victory and success, rather than our past history of failures and setbacks.

Once again, there is much more we could say about memory, and the importance of memorization. If you desire to be strong in Spirit, cultivate this important spiritual faculty.

AGAPE LOVE

The third faculty I wish to explore is the faculty of love. While the world today generally focuses on love as an emotion, the Bible describes love as a spiritual principle that guides and directs the life.[74] Note first, that it is clearly connected with the heart of man: "Now the end [goal] of the commandment is charity out of a pure heart" (I Timothy 1:5). This makes sense, when we remember that the Law of God is in essence a set of

---

74. *There are actually three Greek words for love: Eros, which is a physical attraction. Phileo, which is the emotional enjoyment of another person. And Agape, with is a sacrificial commitment to another's good. While we are focusing on this third kind of love, it is curious that these words can be directly linked to the three compartments of the sanctuary.*

moral principles defining true love. All the commandments are "briefly comprehended in this saying, namely, Thou shalt love thy neighbour as thyself" (Romans 13:9).[75] An even better symbol for love can be found however in the Mercy Seat, the lid on the top of the Ark, which interposed itself between the Shekinah Glory above and the tables of stone below. Much as infinitive love, in the person of Jesus Christ, interposed himself between a holy God and sinful man. That covering over the tables of stone, represents love, for love covers a "multitude of sins" (I Peter 4:8).

Knowing that biblical love (Agape) is not so much a feeling, as a principle, helps us to understand its function. Like conscience and memory, love prompts the mind to do things that are kind and caring to others around us. It inspires us to manifest genuine interest, compassion, and concern. Paul described it this way:

> But as touching brotherly love ye need not that I write unto you: for ye yourselves are taught of God to love one another. And indeed ye do it toward all the brethren which are in all Macedonia: but we beseech you, brethren, that ye increase more and more.
> I Thessalonians 4:9-10

In other words, God is constantly sending impulses to do the loving thing in our varied situations. This is no doubt what Paul meant when he said "the love of Christ constraineth us" (II Corinthians 5:14). When the Spirit comes into our life, it awakens within us impressions to act with genuine Agape

---

75. See also Matthew 22:35-40.

love.[76] "The love of God is shed abroad in our hearts by the Holy Ghost which is given unto us" (Romans 5:5). Our part is to yield to those impressions, and to "increase more and more."

With every prompting however, comes a choice. We can honor the impression, and do what is best for the other person. Or we can put self first, and pursue our own interests and needs. These subtle decisions are made hundreds of times a day, and the choices we make reveal something about the condition of our character.[77] It also influences how we view people.

Suppose for example, you are a young man, and your wife has just had her first baby. It is 3:00 in the morning, and the baby begins to cry. You glance over at your wife, who is sleeping angelically. The thought comes to your mind: "She must be exhausted from taking care of the baby. I should let her get some rest. Maybe I should go check the baby, and try and put it back to sleep."

But then quick on its heels comes another thought: "This bed is so warm and comfortable. I need my rest. I have to go out and work all day. My wife stays home–she should take care of the baby. What does she do at home all day, anyway?" In a matter of seconds your wife is transformed from sweet and angelic to lazy and probably dishonest: laying there just pretending to be asleep! And the entire change took place without her even blinking an eye.

---

76. I Corinthians 13:4-7 gives a whole list of attributes associated with love. Christians would do well to memorize this passage and make a lifelong study of internalizing its principles.

77. "But whoso hath this world's good, and seeth his brother have need, and shutteth up his bowels of compassion from him, how dwelleth the love of God in him? My little children, let us not love in word, neither in tongue; but in deed and in truth." I John 3:17-18.

Of course, the real change took place in you. Your perception of your wife changed dramatically the moment you decided to reject the impression to do what was loving. This is not to say, we should always help every person in every situation. Judgment has to evaluate each impression. There are biblical guidelines that govern when and how we are to help people. But the point is, any time we betray some heaven sent prompting to care for another person, our perception of that person becomes distorted just that little bit. It has to do with the problem of rationalization we have talked about before. We justify and excuse our selfish behavior, thereby blinding ourselves to the reality of the situation. "But be ye doers of the word, and not hearers only, deceiving your own selves" (James 1:22). Sin causes us to lose our ability to see people clearly.

This is the source of most interpersonal conflict. Each person magnifies the faults of the other, and minimizes their own. Both might admit they didn't handle everything exactly right, but the bulk of the responsibility surely lies with the other person. Jesus described this situation in the Sermon on the Mount: "why beholdest thou the mote that is in thy brother's eye, but considerest not the beam that is in thine own eye? . . . Thou hypocrite, first cast out the beam out of thine own eye" (Matthew 7:3,5). In most cases, if either one would simply humble themselves, and sincerely confess their wrongs, the other would respond in kind. Most problems could be resolved in five minutes if we just refused to let pride get in the way!

But pride is a deadly sin, and all too common. It can creep into any relationship: husband, wife, brother, sister, parent, child, co-worker, church member, acquaintance or friend. Even total strangers. Reject the impression of the Holy Spirit to show genuine love to a person, and the mind gets busy transforming that person into something unworthy of love.

They are morphed from a living, breathing person, into an obstacle, or a means to an end. They become little more than objects. Over time, our inclination to show love to anyone diminishes.

True love, in contrast, sees others through the eyes of Christ. As precious, and valuable. As having tremendous potential. Tremendous worth. It inspires us to take an interest in people, to take note of what is important to them, and to search for ways to be a blessing to them. Every act of service, is an investment of treasure in that person. Which only deepens our love for them, for "where your treasure is, there will your heart be also" (Matthew 6:21). By responding to the impressions of the Holy Spirit, we remain free to see people as they truly are: a valuable son or daughter of God. I suspect this is why Jesus said:

> *Resist not evil . . . Love your enemies, bless them that curse you, do good to them that hate you, and pray for them which despitefully use you, and persecute you; That ye may be the children of your Father which is in heaven. Matthew 5:39,44*

To respond angrily is to lose our ability to see them through the eyes of Christ. Blindness settles in. Love becomes crippled.

The goal is to respond to the constraining power of love consistently. To resist self-centered thinking. No matter how fierce the battle, we must immerse every choice in the power of the Gospel. Paul describes what this life looks like, and concludes that it is the essence of being like Christ:

> *Let nothing be done through strife or vainglory; but in lowliness of mind let each esteem other better than themselves. Look not every man on his own things, but every man also on the things of others. Let this mind be in you, which was also in Christ Jesus. Philippians 2:3-5.*

Like our physical eyes and ears, love is a sense organ that enables us to look at people, and listen to them, in new ways. It teaches us how to care for them, as Christ would. It is the secret to filling our lives with loving relationships.

Another book could be written on the topic of Agape love. But it really does boil down to relationships. If you want to experience a more Spirit-filled life, examine your relationships. Is there conflict? Frustration? Resentment? Distance? Apathy? Begin reconnecting with people. Reconcile damaged relationships, and revive neglected ones. Meet new people. And in all your interpersonal interactions, learn to listen to the still small voice of the Holy Spirit, prompting you to show love. It is another vital spiritual faculty. It is how Christ lived his life among men.

FAITH & IMAGINATION

Which brings us to our final spiritual faculty. The faculty of faith. In the Bible, we are told "God hath dealt to every man the measure of faith" (Romans 12:3). That is, every person has some capacity to exercise faith. We may not understand exactly what faith is, or how it works, but it is a part of all of our lives. And it is perhaps the most important of all our faculties.

In the Bible, faith is often closely linked with the other spiritual faculties: "Now the end of the commandment is charity out of a pure heart, and of a good conscience, and of faith unfeigned" (I Timothy 1:5). "Hold fast the form of sound words, which thou hast heard of me, in faith and love" (II Timothy 1:13). "Let us draw near with a true heart in full assurance of faith, having our hearts sprinkled from an evil conscience" (Hebrews 10:22). Consistently faith is described as a function of the heart.

In fact, authentic faith has to be from the heart. An intellectual assent to truth (the mind) is important, but unless truth is received into the heart, by faith–it does not change the life:

> *If thou shalt confess with thy mouth the Lord Jesus, and shalt believe in thine heart that God hath raised him from the dead, thou shalt be saved. For with the heart man believeth unto righteousness; and with the mouth confession is made unto salvation. Romans 10:9-10.*

Change comes to the life when our heart believes. I may be able to answer tough question about some doctrinal topic, but that doesn't mean I've internalized that truth into the core of my being. When the Ethiopian asked Philip, "See, here is water; what doth hinder me to be baptized?", Philip answered, "If thou believest with all thine heart, thou mayest" (Acts 8:36-37). Faith must function from the heart, for it is a spiritual faculty. It is rooted in the Most Holy Place of the temple, though like every other spiritual faculty, it inspires and instructs the mind.

In Hebrews 11, the great faith chapter, faith is actually described much like a sense organ. It begins with this definition: "faith is the substance of things hoped for, the evidence of things not seen" (Hebrews 11:1). It then proceeds to describe various Bible characters who saw some spiritual reality by faith, they could not see with their physical eyes. Noah was "warned of God of things not seen as yet" and prepared himself for the coming flood. Abraham journeyed looking for a city "whose builder and maker is God." Moses endured "seeing him who is invisible" (Hebrews 11:7, 10, 27). In fact this is what they all shared in common. "These all died in faith, not having received the promises, but having seen them afar off, and were persuaded of them, and embraced them" (Hebrews 11:13). They saw them through the eyes of faith.

Without this spiritual faculty, man has little hope of perceiving spiritual truth, regardless of intellect or education. When certain Jews rejected his message, he said the problem was not mental but spiritual. "The heart of this people is waxed gross, and their ears are dull of hearing, and their eyes have they closed; lest they should see with their eyes, and hear with their ears, and understand with their heart, and should be converted" (Acts 28:27). Unbelievers walk "in the vanity of their mind, having the understanding darkened, being alienated from the life of God through the ignorance that is in them, because of the blindness of their heart" (Ephesians 4:17-18). That is, a blind heart leads to a darkened mind. In such situations, the faculty of faith becomes perverted into the faculty of imagination. "When they knew God, they glorified him not as God, neither were thankful; but became vain in their imaginations, and their foolish heart was darkened" (Romans 1:21).

This makes sense, if you think about it. Imagination, like faith is the capacity to see things in our mind that we cannot see with our physical eyes. It is largely drawn from images stored in our memory, connected together in creative and often powerful ways. And imagination, like faith, is clearly connected with the heart. Before the flood, mankind is described in these words: "And GOD saw that the wickedness of man was great in the earth, and that every imagination of the thoughts of his heart was only evil continually" (Genesis 6:5). Two chapters later, after the flood has destroyed the earth, little had changed. "And the LORD said in his heart, I will not again curse the ground any more for man's sake; for the imagination of man's heart is evil from his youth" (Genesis 8:21). In other words, it is as if faith and imagination are really the same faculty. The only difference is that faith dwells on that which is true, and imagination dwells on that which is false. It's more a question of where this faculty is directed.

In my study of the Bible, I have come across more than 30 references to imagination. In virtually every instance, it is used in a negative connotation[78]: men imagining mischief, wickedness, or evil. Or imagining vain things, after their own heart, and against the Lord. In fact, we become "mighty through God" by "casting down imaginations, and every high thing that exalteth itself against the knowledge of God" (II Corinthians 10:4-5). Imagination is the misuse of faith.

Because imagination is a spiritual faculty, it is closely connected to the heart. That is, where the imagination focuses has a direct impact on our character. When a person uses his imagination, for example, to "lust after" a woman, the Bible says, he "hath committed adultery with her already in his heart" (Matthew 5:28). One does not need to commit the act to have a record of the act imprinted in the memory. He only needs to exercise the imagination. This is one reason popular entertainment is so dangerous. By watching sensuality, violence, and other forms of immorality repeatedly, it begins to impress itself on the character, without us having to do a single thing. We are being subtly reprogrammed.[79] The enemy

---

78. The sole exception is I Chronicles 29:18, where David at the end of his life prays God would keep his plans and preparations for the temple in the "imagination of the thoughts of the heart of thy people." That is, that God would grant them a vision to complete the building of the temple. In this instance, he is really talking about faith!

79. Marketers know the effectiveness of this process, for they spend millions on media advertising each year. And we see that success every time we walk down the department store aisle, and our child asks for some brand name item.

understands this principle well, and marshals the most brilliant minds possible to entice our youth into watching countless hours of video, reading fictional novels, playing computer games, and the like. His goal is direct access to the character. Through the imagination, he can bypass all the natural defenses of the mind: the reason, the emotions, and the will. We are transformed by merely participating vicariously.

But if imagination is the wrong use of this faculty, it at least sheds some light on the right use of it. That is, it helps us to understand how faith can mold our character in the proper direction. By consistently focusing the power of faith on the conceptualization of spiritual truths, those truths can also be internalized and imprinted onto the tables of the heart. Stumbling on to the following statement, was a turning point for me in my understanding of faith:

> *As your soul yearns after God, you will find more and still more of the unsearchable riches of His grace. As you contemplate these riches, you will come into possession of them.*[80]

Did you catch that? By engaging that faculty which enables us to contemplate God's unsearchable riches, we come into possession of them. We are transformed. Faith is the capacity to visualize unseen spiritual reality. No doubt this is what Paul meant, when he said "For we walk by faith, not by sight" (II Corinthians 5:7).

---

80. *God's Amazing Grace, p. 187.*

As Christians we need to learn more about how to exercise this faculty. When Jesus taught, He used stories that would call out the imagination. Or in this case, we could say faith, because He was trying to paint a picture of spiritual realities, of truth. In other words, Jesus was speaking more to the spirit than to the mind. Parables such as the lost sheep, the pearl of great price, the mustard seed, and the ten virgins, were all calculated to reveal the mysteries of the kingdom in simple but powerful language. They engaged more than just reason–they engaged the heart. As the two men on the road to Emmaus put it, when describing how Jesus taught, "Did not our heart burn within us, while he talked with us by the way, and while he opened to us the scriptures?" (Luke 24:32). It was this ability to inspire faith and quicken the heart, that made His messages so powerful.[81] We need more preaching and teaching like this today!

We must learn to study the Scriptures with the heart. To fully interact with what we read by faith. To enter into the experience of the passage. The words must move us. Grasp the realities. Use the imagination to embrace every scene. Lay hold of spiritual truth until it burns within the heart. The word of God must be a living, breathing book if it is to impact our life.

The Bible should be seen as a book of grand mysteries. Mysteries that exceed our ability to fully comprehend them. In fact, that is what makes them a "mystery"–the fact they exceed

---

81. *The story is told of a famous actor who was once asked why performers had so much more power over their audiences than preachers: He answered, "We on the stage speak of things imaginary as if they were real, and you in the pulpit speak of things real as if they were imaginary." Quoted in Education, p. 233. No wonder there is so little power in many pulpits!*

the powers of reason. That the heart alone can grasp them. Take the mystery of godliness: God becoming a man. Or the mystery of iniquity: man making himself God. These are profound themes, with profound implications. Inexhaustible implications philosophers have wrestled with for centuries. And the mystery of the resurrection: when mortality puts on immortality, in the twinkling of an eye. Can you imagine what that day will be like? Or the mystery of the Gospel: the power of the resurrection available to me personally, right now, this instant. The cross is a topic we will study throughout eternity and yet never exhaust. These mysteries and many others, fill the pages of the Bible. "O the depth of the riches both of the wisdom and knowledge of God! how unsearchable are his judgments, and his ways past finding out" (Romans 11:33).

We are not talking about things theologians "figure out." Paul said, it was "by revelation [God] made known unto me . . . the mystery of Christ" (Ephesians 3:3,5). God alone can illuminate the heart with the light of His own glory. It is a supernatural work of the Spirit in our heart. These mysteries are truths that must be discerned spiritually. There is no other way to embrace them. They must be received by faith.

And this is where faith can be seen in the Most Holy Place. The awesome mystery of the Shekinah Glory. Just as the two cherubim on either side gaze endlessly into the mysterious visible presence of God, so we too must learn to turn the eye of faith toward Christ. By beholding we will become changed. We will be transformed into the same glorious image. In contemplation of such a mystery, what worldly entertainment compares? All else fades into insignificance in the light of His glory and grace. Lord, grant us faith!

*   *   *   *   *   *   *

The Spirit-filled life is essentially one where all our spiritual faculties are exercised to their maximum potential. When conscience, memory, love and faith are activated by the Gospel, they become channels through which divine grace flows into the life. Our lives become inspired and empowered by the Spirit. It makes following Christ a joy and a delight. "In thy presence is fulness of joy; at thy right hand there are pleasures for evermore" (Psalms 16:11).

Review Questions
Chapter 6–Life in the Spirit

1.   *Explain how our spiritual faculties work. In what ways are they similar to physical senses? How are they different?*

2.   *Summarize what the Bible teaches about the conscience. How can we sensitize our conscience to right and wrong?*

3.   *In what way is memory a spiritual faculty? What can we do to ensure this faculty works properly?*

4.   *Contrast the world's view of love, with that of the Bible. How is this faculty involved in our perception of people?*

5.   *Explain how faith and imagination are similar. What is the connection between faith and the mysteries of Scripture?*

The Quest
Chapter 7

One thing have I desired of the LORD, that will I seek after;
that I may dwell in the house of the LORD
all the days of my life, to behold the beauty of the LORD,
and to enquire in his temple.
Psalms 27:4

In some ways, I feel we have but begun our study. That we have just barely established a framework for talking about all kinds of interesting topics. It is as if we had discovered a whole new "language" we could use to talk about things like marriage and parenting, personal discipleship, mental health therapies, worship and church dynamics, evangelism, and more–but we haven't yet said anything about any of these topics! And as noted in the last chapter, even the topics we have discussed could be greatly expanded. Entire books could be written on any of the faculties we have been able to survey here only briefly. As noted in the preface, what's really needed is a larger community, working together, to fill in the missing pieces of this model, correct mistakes and oversights, and explore the countless implications. This book is just a starting point. Others will hopefully take it much further.

But in another sense, the book is somewhat complete. If only a framework, then it is at least a somewhat comprehensive framework. We've covered all the regions in the nature of man and the main faculties suggested by the sanctuary. The physical and spiritual senses. We've surveyed the mechanics of temptation. The key processes involved in character development. It may be only a sketch, but it is a sketch of the entire system of moral machinery. I can only think of one thing that is missing: a practical plan for taking these insights and integrating them into our personal life.

A PERSONAL QUEST

To be honest, writing this book was something of a personal quest. Several years ago, I went through a traumatic experience in my ministry that deeply impacted my life. While God sustained and sheltered us through that entire experience, my heart was, well, traumatized. Something broke. And it led to various struggles in my life. In hindsight, I see clearly the issue was spiritual: my faith wavered, my conscience became less sensitive, my love waxed cool, and my memory began to dwell on those dark events. Perhaps the incident just revealed longstanding issues in my character I had not seen before. Perhaps it was an attack inspired by the enemy, calculated to destroy my work. More likely, it was a combination of the two. Regardless, it sent me down a path of personal exploration, in pursuit of answers. A quest.

At the time, I had already begun studying the sanctuary. Enough to be convinced it could shed light on the inner struggles of my heart. So I dove in, with six more years of intense study, contemplation, and prayer. At the end of that process, I was more convinced than ever, that the sanctuary gives us a system for understanding man's moral machinery that is at once simple, and yet useful and robust. My goal in writing this book was to somehow make that information more personal. To move it from theory to practice. Not just for others, but for my own life.

In typing out the last few words of the preceding chapter, I had basically finished everything I had planned to write. Yet something still seemed missing: I wasn't sure what it was. I had packaged up all the ideas more neatly than ever before, and had even made a few helpful new discoveries along the way. But what was I supposed to do with the information? It didn't quite feel done. I realized I had yet not completed my quest. So I began to pray about it.

HONEST WITH GOD

Two specific things came to mind. First, the absolute need for raw honesty before God. As noted already, it is one thing to grasp the principles of the moral machinery intellectually, it is another thing to grasp them with the heart. That is, we are dependent on God to truly show us the condition of our own personal sanctuary. Most of us would generally admit to having blind spots, deficiencies, weaknesses. Areas we yield to the flesh or the world, perhaps without wanting to. Times we have rationalized wrong choices, or missed messages from our spiritual faculties. But if someone were to ask us to list several specific examples of each—we might find it quite a challenge. Because we tend to be blind to our own issues, we find it hard to connect Scriptural principles to the day to day details of our life (however accurately we may think we can diagnose problems in others). To truly discover which parts of our sanctuary are not functioning optimally, we must go to God. We must open ourselves up to divine inspection.

Search me, O God, and know my heart: try me, and know my thoughts: And see if there be any wicked way in me, and lead me in the way everlasting. Psalms 139:23-24

Examine yourselves, whether ye be in the faith; prove your own selves. II Corinthians 13:5

Probably the easiest way to do this is to ask yourself pointed questions about the various faculties we have looked at, and then learn to listen prayerfully for the voice of the Spirit of God to give you answers. It cannot be rushed. We must slowly meditate on the various pieces of the moral machinery and give God time to speak to us. It will usually come as a still, small voice, gently working its way through the various layers of our ego defenses. But if we are alert, we can catch the message.

Here are the kinds of questions I'm thinking about. You can read through them quickly now, but to get the full effect, come back later and give it some time. Pray over each question and take time to listen. If you are honest with God, you will soon begin hearing Him speak.

- Are there specific areas where I tend to give in to the desires of my flesh?
- What actions do I engage in that are not in full harmony with Scripture?
- Can I recall incidents where my will seemed powerless to resist temptation?
- Are there rationalizations in my thought life, that I use to justify compromise?
- Do I struggle with specific negative emotions? Which, and what triggers them?
- In what situations or areas am I most likely to ignore the voice of conscience?

- Are the memories that come to mind largely positive or negative? Are they rooted in Scripture?
- Are there specific people you find it difficult to see through Christ's eyes, and love genuinely?
- In what ways am I drawn to vain imaginations, rather than the spiritual realities of faith?

These kinds of questions and others like them give God a chance to speak to our heart, but only if we are willing to face the answers. That's where the raw honesty comes in.

It's also not a one time thing. God only shows us as much about our self as we are ready to deal with at any given time. And some defects in the moral machinery are only discerned in specific situations. Self-evaluation, and raw honesty before God, must be an ongoing part of our Christian experience.

As you begin to see things about yourself, those insights must be combined with action. Reread the appropriate sections of the book. Look for practical suggestions, information about the nitty-gritty, nuts and bolts of how that faculty functions. And then develop a plan. Then put your plan to the test. If one strategy doesn't work, try another. Experiment. Continuously assess your progress, and stick with it.

I thought on my ways, and turned my feet unto thy testimonies. I made haste, and delayed not to keep thy commandments. Psalms 119:59-60

Each person's situation is unique. The Holy Spirit will have to direct you individually how to integrate the principles of the sanctuary into your own life. It will take time, and you will have to persevere. But don't settle for anything less. The moral machinery must become real.

THE POWER OF FELLOWSHIP

The second thing God brought to my mind is the importance of fellowship. The way grace flows to us through brothers and sisters who know us, and can help us to see things about ourselves we might otherwise miss. The blessings God sends through transparency, sharing, and accountability. While God does not need people to show us our defects of character, He often uses them, because our spiritual sensitivities are so dulled in specific areas. These blind spots are sometimes the result of upbringing, education, or culture. At other times, they are the result of our own wrong choices and rationalizations, and the inevitable tuning out of God's corresponding promptings. Either way, God often resorts to using people. "Iron sharpeneth iron; so a man sharpeneth the countenance of his friend" (Proverbs 27:17).

Actually this entire chapter came to me in this way. My wife and I had gotten a little time away to celebrate a milestone in our marriage–a wedding anniversary. I had just finished the first six chapters of the book, and so we took some time to read through them together. As she shared her initial reactions, asked various questions, and pointed out specific observations about my life, I gained several *personal* insights I would have otherwise missed. The sanctuary began to speak. Later that day, I was on the phone speaking with my daughter, and she brought up some questions she was wrestling with in her life. We talked about them together at some length–in the light of the sanctuary. And again, I gleaned some important lessons for myself through that conversation. Reflecting on those experiences, I realized the book was not complete without emphasizing the importance of this kind of interaction. The moral machinery is not designed for hermits. It runs best in the context of genuine fellowship.

*Take heed, brethren, lest there be in any of you an evil
heart of unbelief, in departing from the living God. But
exhort one another daily, while it is called To day; lest
any of you be hardened through the deceitfulness of sin.
Hebrews 3:12-13*

You may wish to consider organizing a small study
group to work through this book with others. Take one chapter
at a time and discuss its content with a focus toward personal
application. Or perhaps it can be used as a resource for prayer
meeting in your church, or as a textbook for the lesson study
time at your church. If possible, combine your review and
analysis of the content with time for sharing and personal
reflection. Often the insights that unlock some area of one
person's life will unlock the same or similar areas in another
person's life. And there must also be time for prayer. Prayer for
more honesty before God. For insight into our true condition.
For grace and power for change. "Again I say unto you, That if
two of you shall agree on earth as touching any thing that they
shall ask, it shall be done for them of my Father which is in
heaven. For where two or three are gathered together in my
name, there am I in the midst of them" (Matthew 18:19-20).

To help you enter into deeper honesty with God, and
closer fellowship with other believers, we are planning to pull
together some companion study guides for this book, designed
to help you build the principles of the moral machinery into
your life. These guides will challenge you to ask tough
questions of God, and then face the answers. They will also
give you tools to encourage personal sharing, learning and
review, and prayer support for one another. If you are serious
about wanting to make the sanctuary system a practical part of

your life, you may want to work through the guides more than once. Each time, you will have the opportunity to review the most important aspects of the sanctuary and find some new way to integrate that information into specific areas of your life. Call for information about the availability of these study guides.

THE QUEST CONTINUES

Well, we have come at last to the end of our study. But not the end of the quest. If you have gotten this far in the book, you have granted my request of at least hearing me out. Thank you for the chance to share some of the wondrous parallels between the sanctuary and man's moral machinery. The three regions in our nature. The various faculties of the body, mind, and heart, and how they interact together. The physical senses and the spiritual senses. The battles that take place every day in our lives, and the power of the Gospel available to help us win them. Keys to transformation of character, and secrets to a Spirit-filled life. We have covered a lot of ground. And I trust you have found the sanctuary to be a valuable model, or map, indeed.

Yes, our study may have come to an end, but the quest continues. I certainly intend to keep learning, growing, seeking. I'm looking for a full restoration of all my physical, mental, and spiritual faculties. My longing is to "be preserved blameless unto the coming of our Lord Jesus Christ" in every area. And I'm thankful for the promise: "Faithful is he that calleth you, who also will do it" (I Thessalonians 5:23-24). The sanctuary is a tool, given by God, so He can dwell with us. In our hearts. His way is there, in the sanctuary. The truths it teaches have revived my heart, and quickened my spirit–but I want more. I can't wait to see what lies ahead for my life as I continue to pursue this journey of becoming like Christ. Won't you come join me in this quest?

> *The temple has been yielded, and purified of sin;*
> *Let Thy Shekinah Glory Now shine forth from within,*
> *And all the earth keep silence, the body henceforth be*
> *Thy silent, gentle servant, Moved only as by Thee.*

Review Questions
Chapter 7–The Quest

1. *What must be combined with the model presented in this book to make it effective in the life?*

2. *Explain how honesty with God is important.*

3. *Why is fellowship so powerful in helping us to understand the moral machinery?*

4. *Which areas of the sanctuary most need development in your personal life?*

5. *What can you do to ensure you continue on in your quest for Christlikeness?*

Appendix
About the Sanctuary

The Old Testament sanctuary was a large tent constructed by the ancient Hebrews shortly after being freed from slavery in Egypt–for the purpose of worship. It was replaced by a majestic building during the reign of King Solomon. That building was destroyed by the Babylonians, rebuilt under Persian rule, and destroyed again by the Romans. Only a portion of the outer wall remains today.

The basic design involved an *Outer Court*, and an inner building. The *Outer Court* was a large enclosure surrounded by a white linen screen containing two pieces of furniture: the *Altar of Burnt Sacrifice* where various offerings were made, and a large *Brass Laver* used by the priests to wash their hands and feet. The building proper was divided into two sections: the *Holy Place*, where priests performed most of their duties, and the *Most Holy Place*, entered just once a year by the High Priest. In the *Holy Place* were three pieces of furniture: The *Table of Shewbread* where priests placed two stacks of cake each week. A seven-branched *Golden Candlestick*, where priests daily trimmed the wicks and replenished the oil. And finally the *Altar of Incense*, where priests burned fragrant spices before the Lord. The *Most Holy Place* was hidden behind a thick curtain and contained but one piece of furniture: the *Ark of the Covenant*. Over this gold chest was a covering called the *Mercy Seat*, and above it, the *Shekinah Glory* hovered, surrounded on either side by two angelic cherubim gazing into its sacred mysteries. The entire sanctuary and all its services communicated profound symbolic meaning. To understand some of that meaning is the purpose of this book.

Map of the Sanctuary

(Not drawn to scale)

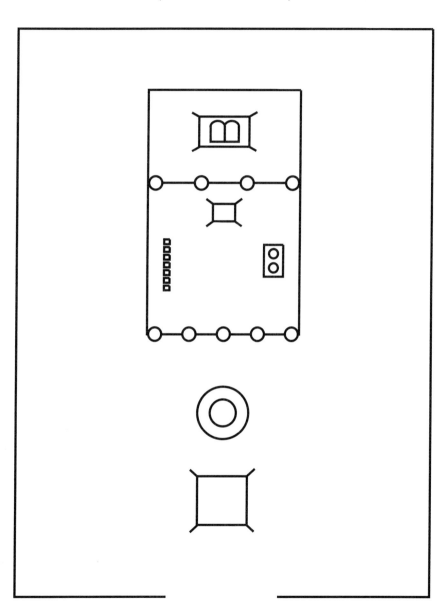

Notes

Notes

FAST Training Resources
Phone: 1-800-501-4024   Web: WWW.FAST.ST

Survival Kit:
Five brief studies for Christians interested in Bible memorization, and our highly effective "Keys to Scripture Memory." Our best introduction to laying up the Word! Includes five lessons, a verse pack, and cards. *$7.00.*

Basic Training:
This challenging program gives practical tools for becoming a more effective disciple. Learn how to build Scripture into every area of life! Includes nine lessons, a verse pack, and cards. *$10.00.*

Team Tactics:
Call your friends to even deeper commitment, by studying Bible secrets to soul-winning. Transform your group into an evangelistic team. Includes nine lessons, a verse pack, and cards. *$10.00*

Leader's Manual:
A small nuts and bolts booklet on how to lead a *FAST* team successfully and encourage others to take in God's Word. *$3.00*

Discipleship Pack:
Want to tackle our complete discipleship curriculum? This pack includes all the materials listed above, including a Leaders Manual. *$30.00*

Memory Packs
Each Memory Pack (M-Pack) comes with 50+ pre-printed cards with choice verses on various topics plus a verse pack and partner's checklist. Ideal for more experienced memorizers. Topics include:

Plan of Salvation:
Covers sin, the Savior, assurance, grace, the Holy Spirit, the lordship of Christ, and more. *$6.00*

Practical Discipleship:
Covers Bible study, memorization, prayer, faith, time management, diligence, and more. *$6.00*

Endtime Events:
Covers signs of the end, prophecies of the Messiah, the Antichrist, the False Prophet, God's final warning, and more. *$6.00*

Basic Bible Teaching:
Covers inspiration, the second coming, death, hell, the law of God, the true day of worship, and more. *$6.00*

Spiritual Leadership:
Covers witnessing, team building, the power of example, faithfulness, spiritual multiplication, and more. *$6.00*

For a complete list of resources, please call or visit our website. Prices subject to change. Shipping and handling not included.

KEY Institute: Check out our challenging web-based training school and take a class with others from around the world. Try our review engine, the card generator, our sword drills, and more. Enroll today at WWW.FAST.ST.